# Hats Off to You

## 2

*Balancing Roles
and Creating Success
in Family Business*

**Ernest A. Doud, Jr.
Lee Hausner, Ph.D.**

Achieving prosperity, harmony,
well-being and balance in every family
and entrepreneurial business today!

We have been truly gratified by the response to the first edition of "Hats Off to You." It has been hailed as:

- "An easy read"
- "Practical"
- "An eye opener"
- Makes good sense

Most important of all the reactions is that the Six Transition model has been credited with helping both business owners, their families and their trusted advisors understand the comprehensive nature of the challenges inherent in succession planning for family business. Put in the context of our model, the succession process is a life-long effort of interconnected transitions that is repeated in every generation.

Our on-going work as strategic advisors to family businesses continues to be a learning experience. Notably, we have learned that the Six Transition model reflects the challenges of family businesses in many countries and cultures around the world. Some of the details in the Ownership and Estate transitions change because of national differences in taxation policies impacting the transfer of wealth from one generation to the next. However, the 6 transitions in the model appear to accurately recognize the categories of challenges faced by family businesses the world over.

Although only three years have passed since the first edition was published, we have gained enough additional perspective to warrant this edition of "Hats Off to You." If you have already read the first edition, you will be particularly interested in the new features of this edition. They include the following:

## Our Latest Thinking About Strategic Planning

In the "Business Transition" chapter of Part II there is an up-dated treatment of strategic business planning. The improvement in the strategic business planning process is just one of the benefits of new perspectives gained as a result of the merger between Doud\Hausner and Associates andVISTAR, LLC that created DoudHausnerVistar.

## Introductory Comments to the Ownership and Estate Transitions

An introduction has been added to the chapters on "Ownership Transition" and "Estate Transition" in Part II. It contains some thoughts about these transitions in light of changes in the Federal estate tax enacted since the first edition was published.

## More Practical Tools

The "PracticalTools" in Part III benefit from some changes and additions. Notably:

- The name of the "Family Assessment Development Questionnaire" has been changed to the "Six Transition Profile." Also, the name of the "Business Assessment Development Questionnaire has been changed to the "Business Prosperity Profile." The content has been revised based on continued experience using this instrument. Extracts of both these instruments are provided as Practical Tool #1.

- A "Personal Well Being Profile" has been added as a third diagnostic instrument. We created this to fill a void. One of the hallmarks of our approach to advising family businesses is our focus on helping clients achieve balance between the three goals common to every family business: Business Prosperity, Family Harmony, and Personal Well Being. The questionnaire we designed to help clients and their advisors define needs and priorities around the first two goals have been very well received. Now we have an instrument that can be used to do the same with the third goal.

- This edition also contains a discussion of the fundamentals of compensation that was not part of the first edition. Compensation is an emotionally charged subject that can be particularly difficult to address in the highly emotional interplay between business and family considerations that exists in most—if not all—family businesses. Understanding the fundamentals of compensation can help families achieve and maintain balance by making responsible decisions about designing, implementing and administering compensation programs.

We trust you will enjoy "Hats Off to You — 2."

Ernie Doud
Lee Hausner

# Introduction

Hats Off to You 2 is widely recognized as one of the premiere books addressing the critical issues that a family must navigate to create a successful, multi-generational family-owned business. The USC Marshall Family Business Program has found this book to be incredibly relevant for our members in achieving our mission statement to *'Create and Preserve Wealth by Increasing the Professionalism of the Business and the Effectiveness of the Family'*. The concepts presented in this book about 'managing your hat collection' and mastering the six critical transitions are so easy to understand, relevant and impactful to both the family and the business.

If you embrace and master the concepts in this book, you will be well on your way to creating a successful, multi-generational family business.

Ken Ude
Director
USC Marshall Family Business Program

**Attention Schools and Corporations:**

Hats Off to You is available at quantity discounts with bulk
purchase for educational, business or sales promotional use.
For information, please call DoudHausnerVistar
at (818) 539-2267.
First Edition published 2000.

Book and Cover Design by Lucy Brown Design,
Santa Barbara, California.

ISBN 1540414884

To share your comments and questions about Hats Off to You,
or to inquire about seminars, workshops and consulting,
please call DoudHausnerVistar at (818) 539-2267
or email edoud@dhvadvisors.com.

# CONTENTS

# DEDICATION

*We dedicate* Hats Off to You — 2 *to four sets of people who are important to us both:*

First, to Maggie, Murray and our children. They have shown remarkable understanding over many years for the long hours, unpredictable schedules and extensive travel that come with the territory in the career we have selected.

Second, to our clients who have been sources of great personal and professional satisfaction, and from whom we have learned so much.

Third, to our colleagues at DoudHausnerVistar who have dedicated themselves to working responsibly and tirelessly on behalf of family businesses.

Fourth, to the many fine advisors in related disciplines with whom we have had the privilege of working. Their technical expertise is admirable, as is their dedication to the success of their family business clients. Because interdisciplinary cooperation is essential when working with family businesses, we particularly appreciate their willingness to cooperate with us.

And last, but by no means least, to the men and women throughout the world who make up the families that own and operate family businesses. Family businesses are, indeed, the backbone of the world economy. Your willingness to accept the risks and challenges posed by all family businesses is to be commended.

The fact that there is a preface to this book is a testament to our ability to reconcile two vastly different points of view—a skill that those involved with family-owned businesses in any capacity would be well served to develop.

When we were formulating the outline for this book, we discovered that Lee always reads a book's preface, whereas Ernie does not. Assuming that those who will read this book might fall into either camp, we were facing a dilemma. If we were to fill the preface with important information, it would be lost to those who don't read prefaces. On the other hand, to omit the preface would be an affront to those who, like Lee, read the preface and look to it to set the tone for a book.

Those who choose to read this will get a brief look at the rationale behind the structure of Hats Off to You —2. For those who, like Ernie, do not read prefaces, you will not see this and will never know what you missed.

Success requires three types of knowledge and information:

- Background
- Perspective
- Practical Tools

We want you to succeed. Therefore, to help you master the succession process in your family business, we have organized this book around these three types of knowledge and information.

Part I provides background knowledge in an Executive Briefing format. It summarizes a fresh view of the subject of family business succession. If, like many busy executives, you have only 10 or 15 minutes to spare, read Part I first.

To build perspective, read Part II. Its six chapters provide in-depth discussions of each of the six family business succession transitions: the Founders, Family, Business, Management, Ownership and Estate Transitions. Chapter 7 sets you on the path to acting on your new perspective.

For guidance in implementation, read Part III. The practical tools and questionnaires on these pages will help you apply your new perspective about family business succession.

*Hats Off to You* —2 provides the background, perspective and practical tools that will help you find "success" in succession planning for your family business.

We have been selective about what we included in this book. We have focused on information used by successful family businesses to answer the most critical succession decisions and resolve the issues that most often get in the way of success.

## What This Book Is (and Is Not)

There is one final piece of business. We will feel more responsible if we let you know what to expect from *Hats Off to You* —2. The following comments will serve to explain and enlighten.

First, expect a book that will add to your insight, broaden your perspective and help create vision. Insight. Perspective. Vision. These are the basic tools you will need to play a leadership role—or a "followership" role—in the succession process in your family business.

Second, expect a book that will focus on what to do more than on how to do it. The insights we have developed in years of working with family businesses have given us the following overviews:

1.  Those of you who have either founded a business or taken the responsibilities of ownership and the reins of leadership from the preceding generation are nobody's fools. You have managed the business successfully and have helped raise your family. You have personally experienced the challenges of juggling the many hats of family business. Those of you who work in a family business or are members of a family that owns and manages a business have also experienced that juggling act. You know first-hand that family businesses can be, simultaneously, enormously satisfying and challenging. Readers who are professional advisors to family businesses endeavor to help their clients find answers to questions and problems that are rarely simple. It takes real dedication to provide

advice that balances the best interests of the business, the family and individual family members. For all of that, *Hats Off to You!*

2.  No individual—nor any one firm of which we are aware—knows it all. To bring this point home, try this: When you are through reading this book, make a list of all the areas in which one would have to have expertise in order to find the balance point for a family business. Your list should include accounting, tax planning, valuation, management consulting, estate planning, financial management and insurance—just to name a few. Then think about yourself, your family, your advisors and all the names in your contact file. See if any individual or firm knows everything one would need to know to do it all. They won't! But between yourself, your family and your team of professional advisors, you probably have access to all the knowledge you need in order to make good decisions and to get things done.

3.  "How to" is not really the issue. The difficulty our clients most often experience is deciding what needs to be done, when and by whom. Therefore, we want to respond to the real issues to help you understand what needs to be done, and how your professional advisors can help with implementation. With that in formation, you and your family can make knowledgeable, informed decisions. (The "how to's" need to be individually determined for each family business. Even if we were tempted to make this a "how to" book, there are just too many possible choices of things to do and too many ways to do them. If we did include all the "how to s," the resulting book would be so thick that we doubt anyone would read it.)

Now that you know what to expect, you can make an informed decision about whether or not to turn the page.

# HOW TO GET THE MOST OUT OF THIS BOOK

## Who This Book is For

If you are part of a family business, *Hats Off to You* —2 should be mandatory reading for every family member.

If you are the founder or current generation leader of a family business, read *Hats Off to You* —2 to gain additional perspective that will make you s of the roles you must play to help ensure the perpetuation of the business into the next generation.

If you are a member of the next generation of leadership and management in your family business, read this book to become a more productive member of the transition team. You will be better prepared to assume leadership and management responsibilities in your generation.

If you are a family member who is not active in the family business, read this book to develop an understanding of the challenges facing those who are. It will position you to contribute as part of the support system that families must be if your family business is to be successfully perpetuated.

If you are a professional advisor serving family business clients, readthis book to better understand the world in which your clients live. Invite every member of your firm to do the same. No matter your professional discipline, the information in *Hats Off to You* —2 will enable you to provide better advice and counsel.

## How To Read This Book

This is not a long book, so ideally one would simply sit down and read it front to back, cover to cover. But knowing that most of our readers already have schedules that would fill a 28 hour day, we thought it prudent to suggest an alternative approach.

**Step 1:** Now that you've purchased *Hats Off to You* —2, if you cannot start reading it immediately, put it on top of your desk or in your briefcase. It will be readily available when you have a few free minutes in the office, or while you are on a plane or train. In any event, don't put it on the bookshelf until everyone in your family has read it!

**Step 2:** When you do start, read Part I in detail. It is an executive briefing that will give you the essence of the message in a few pages.

**Step 3:** Read the two pages at the beginning of Part II titled "Just a Few Words," then scan the body of Part II. This is the "guts" of the book that will provide detailed perspective on an innovative comprehensive approach to family business succession.

**Step 4:** If you are reading for general knowledge, go back and read each chapter in Part II one at a time. Read them in order because each transition in the family business succession planning process builds on those preceding it. If you are in the middle of a problem with one of the transitions, then read it now and go back to the others later.

**Step 5:** Review the Practical Tools that comprise Part III. These tools are intended to be resources you and your family can use in planning and implementing the Six Transition family business succession process.

**Step 6:** Share *Hats Off to You —2* with another member of your family or your firm.

## When To Read This Book

The short answer is to read it right now!

Read it the minute you begin to think about planning for succession in your family's business. The information contained in *Hats Off to You —2* can help you avoid the pitfalls that have caused so much trouble for so many other family businesses.

Read it if you are in the middle of a succession process that is not going as smoothly as you would like. The contents of this book can show you how to resolve the conflicts that have arisen, and make the rest of the succession process smoother and more effective.

Read it if your family business is floundering in the aftermath of an unsuccessful attempt at succession planning. What you learn can help calm the waters.

PART I

**Background /
Executive Briefing**

We have had the opportunity to give many speeches and seminars about and for family businesses. In addition, we have been consultants to hundreds of businesses and the families that own them. It has been personally fulfilling to be both guide and teacher to those who live in the world of the family business. But perhaps the most valuable benefit of our interaction with family businesses is the opportunity to be not only guide and teacher but to take the role of student as well. Thanks to our clients, and to their advisors in other professional disciplines, we have been exposed to many valuable learning experiences over the years. Four of the most important lessons we have learned provide a new perspective to businesses owned by families. Our desire to share those lessons is the reason we wrote this book.

---

### LESSON ONE

#### *Manage your hat collection!*

---

The idea for our title started with the true (and, by now, legendary) story of a business owner, one of his sons and the owner's two hats.

The son entered the family business and was given a unit of the business to run. Unfortunately, his performance was not up to standard, and he had not responded to feedback about this issue.

Invited to his parents' house one evening, he found his father in the spa. On the deck beside him were two baseball hats. The father explained to his son how tough it was being the leader of a family business. On the one hand, he was a parent who cared very much for his children. On the other hand, he was a business executive who cared deeply about his business.

He then donned one of the hats. On the crown of the first hat was the word "Boss." Wearing the Boss hat, he told his son that the business could not tolerate his substandard performance. He handed his son his termination notice and severance check and fired him.

Having delivered that tough message, he immediately changed hats. The word "Dad" was on the crown of the second hat. With his Dad hat on, he put his arm around his son and said, *"I understand you just lost your job. Is there anything Mom and I can do to help?"*

This story is a clear illustration of a dilemma facing everyone in a family business: which hat to wear when facing a tough decision that can involve more than one of the roles you play in the family and the family business.

In the above illustration the CEO was dealing with two hatsl—one as the "Boss" and one as a "Dad." In reality, however, there are not two but at least 15 hats representing the major roles any individual might play in a family and that family's business.They include: Founder, Owner, Chief Executive, Manager, Nonmanagement Employee, Director, Dad, Mom, Spouse, Son or Daughter, Sibling, In-law, Aunt, Uncle and Cousin. And therein lies a big problem: Too many hats and too many choices!

There are four questions everyoneone in a family-owned business should be asking of themselves when a decision with business and/or family implications must be made:

1. What kind of a decision am I making?
   *"Is it ownership? Governance? Management? Parental?*
2. Do I "own" the right hat?
   *"Do I have the right to be involved in the decision in the first place?"*
3. Am I wearing the right hat?
   *"Am I prepared to act in the role that will enable me to make this decision from the right perspective?"*
4. Do I have a voice or a vote?
   *"Do I have/share the responsibility to make the decision, or do I only have the opportunity to give input to the decision makers?"*

---

### LESSON TWO

---

***Everyone in every family business is seeking the same three goals.***

---

## Prosperity, Harmony and Well-Being

Over the years our experience has led us to the realization that everyone in a family business shares three common goals with everyone else in that family and business: (1) business prosperity, (2) family harmony and (3) personal well-being.

Even with this common ground as a foundation, those three objectives often appear impossible to attain simultaneously. Although working to reach all three goals can be frustrating, they are not mutually exclusive.

The solution path gets easier when we understand the principles that strengthen and enlighten any family or entrepreneurial business.

Family-owned businesses are truly part of the American dream. Ernie contributed to the book *Your Family Business: A Success Guide to Growth and Survival,* Some impressive statistics were cited in that book, and we have no reason to believe they have changed since. Fully 90 percent of all the businesses in this country are family owned. If you add the publicly held businesses that are family controlled that number swells to 95 percent and includes about one-third of the Fortune 500. It is clear that family- owned or controlled businesses contribute substantially to our economy.

> ### This is why business prosperity is important.

We also know that most business founders dream that their businesses will create a legacy from which the entire family can benefit.The founder s dream includes the hope that the family will be able to cooperate in such a manner that ownership and management of the business will continue into future generations.

> ### This is why family harmony is important.

Another challenge is the definition of personal well-being. Everyone has a different definition of well-being for himself or herself, in the same way that everyone has a unique thumbprint. If any member of a family believes that his or her personal well-being is being ignored, then that person will act defensively. When we feel backed into a corner, we tend to get tunnel vision. Our survival instincts take over and the interests of the other members of the family and the family as a whole are disregarded.

> ### This is why personal well-being is important.

The hard reality of family businesses is that only about 25% of them survive to the second generation. Of additional concern is that only about 13% ever make it to the third. These statistics suggest that without planning strategically for succession, family businesses are part of an endangered species.

> ### This is why balance is important.

## *Seek and maintain balance between prosperity, harmony and personal well-being*

Our clients and audiences have found our approach to prosperity, harmony and personal well-being both important and informative. These three qualities plus balance are the keys to success in any family business. Helping you discover how to gain your balance is why we wrote this book. Whether you are a family member, work in a family business or act as a professional serving a family business, we are confident that you will come to understand more about the family business world. That understanding can help you make decisions that will support successful family business transitions.

**The Goal: Family and Business—A Powerful Combination**

Family businesses own many intangible assets, including:
- Commitment
- Long-term perspective
- Knowledge
- Loyalty
- Sense of history, continuity and legacy
- Opportunity for family connectedness
- Stable culture
- Reliability
- Pride

These are the resources needed for mastery of the Six Transitions, which you'll learn more about in Part II. The best way to tap their full value is to use them in an environment in which the often conflicting demands of **business prosperity, family harmony** and **personal wellbeing** are in **balance**.

These assets are needed to offset the liabilities often found in any family business:
- Failure to adapt the existing business to change
- Failure to manage family/business dynamics
- Failure to professionalize the management team
- Failure to resolve ownership issues
- Failure to engage in open, honest communication

- Failure to complete planning the estate transfer
- Failure to resolve interpersonal conflicts

We know that these liabilities represent the principal reasons many family businesses fail. However, we also know from experience that these liabilities can be overcome by:

1. Purposeful employment of the family business assets previously listed

2. The willingness of family members to develop strategies to overcome these liabilities.

---

## LESSON FOUR

### *Well-balanced family businesses are unbeatable!*

---

### The Business of Balance

The best way to approach the concept of balance is to have a mental image of it. Imagine an equilateral triangle that is on a horizontal plane and is resting on a pinpoint. It should look something like the graphic below:

Once you have that mental image, place all the members of your family on the top side of the triangle. Next, imagine that the people on the triangle are in constant movement among all three sides trying to keep the triangle balanced. If you can visualize this setting, then you have a creative glimpse into the world of the family business.

But just in case you are not a visual person, we will explain what this mental image is all about. It is about a balancing act in which all family members are the performers. The sides of the triangle represent the three things they must keep in balance if they are to be successful in their family/business relationship:

- Business prosperity
- Family harmony
- Personal well-being

## Why Business Prosperity?

The answer to the need for business prosperity is fundamental. The business is the engine that generates most—if not all—of the wealth for the family that owns it. A prosperous business throws off some very significant benefits:

- A comfortable, economically advantaged lifestyle for the family
- An economic legacy
- A comfortable retirement for today's owners and managers
- Jobs and income for tomorrow's managers
- An asset base for tomorrow's owners
- Career options for qualified family members
- Job and income security for all employees
- Pride in a job well done
- Stature in the industry and community

Who wouldn't want all that?

## Why Family Harmony?

> ### Businesses come and businesses go, but families are forever!

That is one reason family harmony is so important. We are each a part of our family system for life and the family will be there long after we're gone. If we are—in effect—serving a "life sentence" in our family, then life will be much more tolerable if we get along with our family members. If we are lucky enough to actually enjoy each other's company and look forward to being together as a family, then life can be much more than tolerable. It can be fun!

> ### When the family is in conflict, the family's business is adversely affected!

This is the second reality behind the importance of family harmony. If we can't find ways to work together and enjoy each other in the family setting, then imagine what our lives in the family's business will be like:

1. Sooner or later, family discord spills over into the business and vice-versa.

2. This pattern becomes a vicious circle that feeds on itself and be comes more and more intense with time.

We have seen too many instances in which disharmony in the family has caused the business bubble to burst. The economic engine breaks down and is no longer able to supply the advantages associated with prosperity.

## Why Personal Well-Being?

Each person in a family business has the absolute right to seek his or her own model for personal well-being, the absolute right to ask, "What s in it for me?" If everyone arrived at the same definition of personal well-being, then life would be easy.

If only it were so. Reality in family business works out in a slightly different way. Compare the components of your definition of personal well being with those of other family members. You will find that they will vary from being slighdy different to being 180 degrees apart. They will be different for any number of reasons, the most obvious of which are:

- Some family members are owners and others are not.
- Some are actively involved in the business and others are not.
- Some are on the cusp of retirement, some are just starting their careers and still others are somewhere in between.
- Some are married, and others are single.
- Some are willing to accept business and investment risk, while others are risk averse.
- Some are growth investors and others are income investors.
- Some are workaholics and others seek balance between their work and their personal lives.

And the list goes on.

## The Secret Behind Balance

Take a moment to reestablish the mental image you captured earlier. It is the picture of your family in continuous motion about the top of the horizontal triangle that is supported by a pinpoint. They are working to find that one magical, mystical point of perfect balance—and trying very hard not to fall off in the process.

The secret of achieving balance is simple. All you have to do is simultaneously solve two problems and follow one rule. The bad news is that failure to solve the problems and follow the rule will make it virtually impossible for you to find the balance point. The good news is that it is within you and your family's combined power to solve the problems. All you have to be is committed.

## The Two Problems and the One Rule

The first problem to be solved is the matter of balancing family interests with business interests. On the surface they are not always the same. Answers to problems that appear best for the business may not seem best for family interests and vice-versa. The challenge is to find the answers that are best for both the business and the family. It simply means you have to be more creative in developing options to create win/win situations. In part II, chapters 1, 2 and 3 cover the Founder's, Family and Business Transitions that begin that process.

The second problem is reconciling all those different definitions of personal well-being. Can each family member have what he or she wants? Only if each individual is willing to examine and adjust his or her definition of personal well-being in light of all the definitions taken together. The information in chapters 4, 5 and 6, which deal with the Management, Ownership and Estate Transitions, will make solving the second problem a bit easier.

Then there is that little matter of the one rule to be followed.

> *You must never stop trying to achieve balance,*
> *even after you think you have it.*
> *The minute you stop, you'll lose it.*

Simultaneous equations. Lessons. Rules. There seems to be so much to remember! It is much like learning to play golf. Position your feet correctly. Square your shoulders. Keep your head down and your eye on the ball. Get the correct grip. Make sure your back swing is complete. Follow through. And if you do all that just right, then—not always, but more often than not—you will get off a good shot.

Can it be done in golf? Of course! Just watch the pros.

Can it be done in family business? Absolutely! Just talk to anyone in a third-, fourth-, fifth-, or nth- generation family business. You'll find that they have achieved the type of balance we are describing. And you will also find that they never take their family business balance for granted. They are in constant motion on top of the triangle. But instead of rushing around madly, the people involved in successful family businesses are moving purposefully between business prosperity, family harmony and personal well-being.

The stakes are high. It is hard, demanding, never-ending work. Nevertheless, we believe the rewards are definitely worth the effort

> **Balance is what this book is all about.**

PART II

*Perspective*

# JUST A FEW WORDS...
## THE SIX TRANSITIONS MODEL

We built the Six Transitions model to provide a framework for understanding the challenges the family team must resolve at critical transition stages if they hope to find the "success" in family business succession. They are the six most important elements of a family business succession cycle that is repeated in each generation. As you can see from the model on page 27, they have a unique relationship to one another.

**Why are they connected?** The Six Transitions are connected because each depends on the other.

**What makes the Founder's and Family Transitions different from the other four?**
- The Founder s and Family Transitions are enabling transitions that impact each of the other four individually—and all four together. Tend properly to these two transitions and the four implementation transitions become easier. If you ignore the Founder's and Family Transitions, you will find that the four implementation transitions will be very difficult to complete effectively.
- The Business, Management, Ownership and Estate Transitions are implementation transitions. They are the actions you take to make sure the mechanics of succession are in place.

### How to Use the Six Transitions
The utility of the Six Transitions model can vary. It depends on where you are in the succession process.
- If you and your family are beginning to think about succession in your family business, understanding these Six Transitions will help you make better decisions.
- If you are already well into the process, understanding these Six Transitions will enable you to test the soundness of the decisions you have made. As a result, you will be able to make mid-course corrections if needed.

- If you are in a family business in which the succession decisions have all been made and implemented, understanding these Six Transitions will improve the way you and your family play the hand you have been dealt.

# THE SIX TRANSITIONS
## "Balanced" Succession
## in Family Businesses

| FOUNDER | | | |
|---|---|---|---|
| Business | Management | Ownership | Estate |
| FAMILY | | | |

*"All right, ' said the (Cheshire) Cat;*
*and this time it vanished quite slowly,*
*beginning with the end of the tail,*
*and ending with the grin,*
*which remained some time*
*after the rest of it had gone. "*

LEWIS CARROLL
*Alice's Adventures in Wonderland*
1865

## CHAPTER ONE

### *The Founder's Transition*

In first-generation family businesses, keeping the family business dream alive—finding "success" in family business succession—starts with the founder and his or her transition. This transition is equally important in second-and-third generation family business, and beyond. Please note that although we call this the Founder's Transition, most of the concepts we discuss apply to the transition of the current leader in any generation. We elected to use the term "founder" as a matter of convenience.

We have made this the starting point of our Six Transitions model because, of the two enabling transitions, the Founder's Transition is the "gatekeeper" transition of the entire family business succession process.

> **If the founder (or current leader) is not prepared to make a graceful exit, planning for and implementing the remaining transitions can he a frustrating proposition**

Therefore, a successful Founder's Transition is important to you whether you are:
- The founder of a first-generation family business
- The leader of a family business that is in a later generation
- A candidate to be tomorrow's leader
- Someone who works for the founder or current leader, or
- A family member who is not involved in the business

The Founder's Transition is a very timely subject for an ever-growing number of family businesses. A study conducted by Arthur Andersen cited 1952 as the median year for family business formation in the United

States. Therefore, as founders age, an increasing number of businesses are finding that planning for and implementing the Founder s Transition are issues with some immediacy attached.

Ideally, this transition is really a lifetime process. Unfortunately, in practice it is most often not confronted until the later stages of the founders business career or, worse, in the aftermath of a crisis, e.g., the death or disability of the founder. If you fall into that category, take heart in being part of the majority. Keep in mind that it is not too late to use these ideas to improve the quality of the Founder s Transition. If you are a founder who is reading this in early or mid-career, congratulations. You have a head start. And if you are simply an interested bystander to the Founders Transition, the perspective you develop can help you be a positive force in a vitally important process.

### The Founder's Dream

Once upon a time the business founder had a dream, and that dream became the family business. If you are a business founder, chances are you started the business for one or more of the following reasons:

- You saw an opportunity that was too good to pass up, but were constrained by an employer who didn't share your vision or enthusiasm.
- Working for someone else was frustrating and you desperately wanted to be your own boss.
- The rigidity, formality and bureaucracy of a large business was just not your cup of tea.
- Despite contributing to business success, there was no opportunity for ownership and/or you determined that nobody ever "got rich" working for someone else. And for most founders or leaders in family businesses, the idea of continuing the legacy —of handing the baton to the next generation—became part of the founder s dream.

Or perhaps you fell heir to an established business and have been successful in guiding that enterprise to growth and increased profitability. If so, a tradition of keeping the business in the family is already established. Most family business leaders we've met take as a starting point the idea that the tradition should be continued into the next generation.

Founder or current leader—either way, now you can look back with pride and satisfaction at the results of your willingness to take risk, to work hard and to engage in self-sacrifice along the way. It has been an exciting ride, but succession is a matter of "when" and "how best," rather than "if." Knowing that the transition is inevitable, what can you do to make it satisfactory for yourself, your spouse, your family and your business?

Even if the founder is no longer present, his or her influence is very likely still felt to some degree in both the business and the family. More than one of our clients has expressed the belief that one responsibility of family business leadership is keeping the founder's dream alive. And that sentiment has been expressed not just by second generation members but by individuals in the third and fourth generations—and beyond. Much like the Cheshire Cat in *Alice's Adventures in Wonderland*, the tail may have vanished long ago, but the founder's grin lingers on.

## Essential Elements of the Founder's Transition

One of the reasons so few people play really great golf is that it is too complicated. There are just too many "have to's" to remember—let alone execute effectively every time. The same is true of any of the Six Transitions. A friend explained his approach to the game of golf. He finally decided that he couldn't perfect it all, so he worked on what he decided were the essential elements of very good golf. He adopted the philosophy that he didn't need to be a perfect golfer to be successful and have fun. Being very good would be good enough.

We have applied that philosophy to each of the Six Transitions. One need not be perfect. In fact, perfection is probably beyond reach. Being very good will work quite well. And being very good at the Founder's Transition starts with learning and mastering these essential elements.

#1. Understanding the evolution of the founder's role
#2. Deciding what life will be like after the business
#3. Transferring power effectively
#4. Achieving financial independence

## Element #1: Evolution of the Founder's Role

You may not have realized it, but the Founder's Transition has been going on since the day the business began. Chances are that the roles of the founder or leader of the business today have changed somewhat over time as the business has changed. The model that can add individual perspective to this concept is shown on the next page.

| Business Stage | Founder's Roles |
|---|---|
| Start-up | Initiator/Doer |
| Growth | Builder/Student |
| Professionalization | Manager/Teacher |
| Maturity | Mentor/Door Opener |

We will more fully explain the business stages in chapter 2 on the Business Transition. Right now let's focus on the Founder's Transition and the founders roles. This model represents the ideal, which means few people will fit the model exactly. But it is a good test of whether the evolutionary part of the Founder's Transition is progressing as it should.

**Initiator/Doer:** In the beginning of a start-up business, the founder had two principal roles—Initiator and Doer.

The Initiator's challenge is to get the doors open. This includes designing the products and services the business will provide, developing the business plan, selling the idea to funding sources, defining the organization, finding employees and finding customers. As an Initiator, the founder is the idea person, the visionary, the risk taker, the person with the commitment to make it work.

As the Doer, the founder is everywhere: an operations executive and often a production worker, the sales force, the purchasing agent, and head of finance and administration. In a very real sense for a start-up business, the business is the founder and the founder is the business.

**Builder/Student:** There comes a point in time when the business ceases to be a start-up and begins to behave like a growth company. Concurrently, the founder should be making a transition into two new roles. To effectively lead a growth company, the founder needs to become both a Builder and a Student.

Based on what we know of our clients' experiences, neither of these transitions is very difficult. Becoming a Builder involves just a modest modification of the Initiator role. It involves planning for and acquiring resources to support growth (more money, more people, additional space and equipment), and employing those resources effectively.

A growth business is not only building sales volume. It is also becoming larger and more complex internally. When the founder realizes that he or she can't be everywhere at once, it is time to become a Student. We don't mean going back to class for another degree. Rather, this is the time to focus on honing selected skills.

Ideally, these would be the areas the founder enjoys the most—those pursuits at which he or she would prefer to spend more time. In practice, the choice may be dictated by the needs of the business. One founder we know provided some insight into how he made the choice. He said, *"From the beginning I was a great salesman. I had been there before. But I was weaker in financial management than I could afford to be. We were still too small to have our own financial executive. I never thought I could learn so much about finance in such a short time, but I had to."*

Longer-term perspective may dictate other learning choices. Another founder told the following story. *"When I worked for a big company we had a raft of computer experts, so I never paid much attention. One day I realized that the longer-term future of my business depended on how well we used computers. I didn't need to become a systems expert, but I did need to learn enough to make good decisions about how we use the experts we hire."* In the role of Student, the founder builds those skills, which must be enhanced at the time in order to help assure business success and perpetuation.

The farther the business goes in its life cycle, the more complex it becomes. Years ago a colleague introduced us to a useful law:

> ### BRIEN'S SECOND LAW OF BUSINESS
> *Sooner or later, the ability of any business to succeed in spite of itself runs out!*

We don't know who Brien is. We don't even know if there is a first law. But we found the second to contain valuable insight. One interpretation of this law is that there comes a time for every business when informal, seat-of-the-pants management needs to give way to more systematic, "professional" approaches to running the business.

The transition from a growth business to a professionally managed firm can be a struggle because the required transition in roles at this stage is challenging for most founders. The roles of Initiator, Builder and Doer are relatively easy. Becoming a Student is borne of necessity. But becoming a professional manager? This represents a major shift to a role that few founders find very enjoyable. In fact, the skills required of a professional manager may not be part of the founder's skill set.

**Manager/Teacher:** To assume the Manager role, a founder must leverage himself or herself through others. By now the business is sufficiently complex to have outstripped any one person's ability to manage every element of the operation. It probably has at least a budding management team. It is time to delegate, and that means it is time to trust others with the details so the founder can attend to the bigger picture issues.

This creates a two-part dilemma. Part one is that the bigger the business gets, the more details need to be managed. But many entrepreneurs are big-picture types who find details excruciating. Part two of the dilemma is that, although delegation is the expedient answer, most founders don't delegate well. Delegation requires trust, but trust is an attribute that many entrepreneurial founders have difficulty developing.

In a November/December 1985 Harvard Business Review article entitled "The Dark Side of Entrepreneurship," Manfred F.R. Kets deVries states: *"What makes some entrepreneurs I have known stand out as extreme examples has been their strong distrust for the world around them. They live in fear of being victimized. They want to be ready to divest or strike."*

The transition into the role of Teacher is equally confounding. It is a popular conception that entrepreneurs are born, but managers are made. Management requires a set of learned skills, and "the science of management" is a popular term. Assuming the founder decides to delegate—and that may be a big assumption—the obvious challenge is whether the founder can teach. The less obvious challenge lies in the question "Teach what?"

One can be reasonably sure that the founder knows his or her business inside and out but may not have the skills needed to transfer that knowledge to others in ways they can use. To complete the transition to the role of Teacher, the founder should consider the following five questions:

1. What do my managers need to know about the business?
   *Have I, the founder, communicated a vision? Do managers know how I measure business success?*

2. Is the big-picture person, the impatient perfectionist, really ready to effectively transfer to others my perspective about this business?
   *Am I willing to take the time needed to prepare and communicate a concise, objective view of this business as I see it? Am I open to listening and considering different points of view?*

3. What do my managers need to know about managing?
   *Has the company undertaken a comprehensive review of the management process? Is there a model of what it should be and the skills managers need to make that process work? Is there an accurate inventory of individual skills and development needs?*
4. Where and from whom can managers best learn the management skills they need?
   *Which aspects of managing do I know best? In what areas am I weak? What can I teach the managers? What can they best learn from others? Who and where are the "others"?*
5. How much time should be devoted to teaching?
   *How do I find time to teach? Managers are busy, too. How do we make time for them to learn?*

The role of Teacher can be fulfilled in more ways than one. It may very well be that the best use of the founder is not always as a Teacher, per se, but as a Dean of the Faculty—orchestrating the efforts of other teachers.

**Mentor/Door Opener:** The last two roles required of the founder are that of Mentor and Door Opener. Becoming a Mentor is a refinement of the Teacher role. The role of Door Opener is all about letting go —gracefully.

Mentoring is the process of observing and helping others refine the knowledge and skills they learned during the teaching phase. As such, it differs from teaching, which is transmitting the information students need to build basic knowledge and skills.

In the context of the Founder's Transition in family businesses, the Mentor is preparing his or her successor to assume responsibility for the strategic leadership of the business. This requires patience, encouragement and the art of constructive criticism. It also requires the ability to recognize and nurture talents of the designated successor(s), which may differ from those of the founder. Those who have been through it will attest to the fact that the only thing harder than simultaneously being a parent and a boss is being a parent, a boss and a good mentor.

One of the reasons that working outside the family business is so important for successors is that they have a better chance of learning and of accepting mentoring in a more neutral work environment. Within the family business, heirs are often either overly and unfairly criticized or excused for their incompetence. Even reporting to a nonfamily executive is not necessarily a good solution. That individual may have difficulty being fully honest with and about an individual who someday may be the boss.

Perhaps the most important key to a successful mentoring experience is the ability of the mentor to motivate the person in his or her charge. This is accomplished by understanding the critical formula for motivation:

> **Balance is what this book is all about.**

How does this apply to succession within the family business? Positive feelings about the family business begin with the messages the next generation hears and the ways in which they encounter the family business during their formative years. Throughout their lives, children receive messages about the family business in many ways. (They may not be messages we intend to send, but they come through loud and clear.)

- Through listening, they will learn that the business is either
- a source of satisfaction or of continual stress. It is probably both from time to time, but people often focus on problems and challenges. As a result, many children only hear the negatives and form negative impressions of the business.
- Through experience, children will either learn that Mom and Dad's business responsibilities can be balanced with family time, or that the children must compete with the business for their parents' time and attention. In the latter case, the business becomes an envied sibling with whom they must compete for attention.
- Through observation, children will either see the family as united in their business endeavors and able to manage disagreements, or they will see and feel the emotional distress that accompanies unresolved conflicts.
- Children will either be exposed to the business in positive ways that are appropriate for their age at the time, or they will be excluded and the business will remain a mystery.

The key word in the last example is "positive." In the movie Avalon, the film makers present a scene in which one of the principal third- generation characters happily accompanies his father on door-to-door sales calls exhibiting a sense of pride as he carries one of his father's sample cases. By inference, that early experience played a role in the boy's decision to continue in the family business as an adult. It doesn't always work that way. The following story illustrates a breakdown in the "positive feelings" part of the motivation equation.

A "next-generation" member in a client family business (we'll call him "Alan") recounted his experiences with exposure to the business. Alan was often brought to the factory at an early age. His father proudly showed him around, so that Alan knew what went on there and how Dad spent his time. That was all very positive. However, as Alan got older and his intellect grew, he became inquisitive. He was interested in the business and wanted to know how things worked and why they worked that way.

Alan wanted his exposure to the business to evolve as he matured. But although Dad delighted in showing Alan "what," he never permitted him to learn "how" and "why." Although Alan was more than willing to contribute to the success of the family business, his father would not let him assume any responsibilities that would be fulfilling to him. And when he tried to learn from other employees, Dad's response was that they were busy and should not be bothered. Dad assumed a "look but don't touch" philosophy.

The result of this young man's frustrating experience was that by the time he became an adult, he lost interest in a career in the family business. The father-son relationship was strained by arguments with Dad. In virtually every heated exchange, Dad angrily expressed his disappointment that Alan had not developed the interest and business expertise his father assumed he should after all this exposure.

Finally, we look at the founder as a Door Opener. The role of the Door Opener is to transition key relationships to the successor(s). This process sends a clear message about the future of business leadership to employees, customers, suppliers, industry contacts and professional advisors. Succeeding in this role requires that the founder (or current leader) be prepared to make a graceful exit from the business. The most critical positioning components for the founder's exit strategy are the subjects of the remainder of this chapter.

### Element #2: Is There Life After Business?

Most founders and current leaders devote their lives to their businesses—often to the exclusion of other interests. People who become this involved often find it very difficult to envision a meaningful existence outside the context of total involvement in their business. For them, the meaning of their life takes on the attributes of an all-or-nothing proposition. But there are other options.

Fred's real love was new products. He had been responsible for designing the company's first core products before the business became so complex that a research and development department was established. At this stage in the company's evolution, there were two very competent next-generation family members eager to assume more significant management responsibilities. Indeed, they were pressuring Fred (subtly and not-so-subtly) to divest himself of day-to-day operating management responsibilities. However, Fred wanted a continuing role in the business that was more active and involved than serving as chairman of the board. The answer took some time to discover but was enormously rewarding for both Fred and the business. This founder became a consultant to the head of R&D. In effect, he was ending his career right where he started—doing that which he loved most.

Nancy, another founder, was not a detail person. She characterized herself as a strategic thinker, and everyone agreed. Nonetheless, during much of her career she had forced herself to handle the details that come with the job of a chief operating officer. It was not her favorite role, but the one she believed the business needed her to play. When one of her "children" was ready and eager to assume the role of COO, Nancy focused her time and energy on strategic business planning. Now the business has a competent and committed top-level executive serving as its strategic-planning champion. She is delighted, and the business has thrived by making more effective use of her skills and interests.

We offer these real-life examples to stimulate your creative thinking and change your thoughts about "retirement" being the all-or-nothing proposition you may have feared it to be.

## Element #3: Effective Transfer of Power

One of our amusing recollections is of a family business in which the reins of control had purportedly been transferred to the next generation. The founder had been "retired" for a couple of years but continued to come in to the office on a regular basis. During these visits he would assert the power he said he had transferred, giving orders and making pronouncements just like the "good old days." To the founder, this was his right. To his successors, these random activities were disruptive to their efforts to move the business forward under their leadership.

At times like this, a well-developed sense of humor often helps maintain perspective. That became obvious when one of the successors explained: *"Dad is more or less retired. The only trouble is that we never know which day is 'more' and which is 'less.'"*

To illustrate some ways in which founders and leaders approach the transfer of power, Jeffrey Sonnenfeld, author of *The Hero's Farewell: What Happens When CEOs Retire*, describes four departure styles. You can probably identify with at least one of them:

**Monarchs** rule with an iron fist until they are forced out of office by death or palace revolt. As you might imagine, this approach has the potential for substantial disruption of business prosperity, family harmony and personal well-being. We suggest you look at it this way: You can die in the saddle, but it is very hard on the horse.

**Generals** leave, but grudgingly and usually under pressure. Once gone, they engage in two pursuits. First, they spend time with other generals plotting their return. Second, they stay in close enough contact with the business to catch their successor's first mistake. They then parachute back in and "save" the business.

**Governors** serve for a limited term. Once gone, they cut all ties to the business and go on to other endeavors, which may even include starting another business. Successors like the sound of this style until they realize that when the "Governor" left, he took all his knowledge and contacts with him.

**Ambassadors** represent the ideal. They plan their departures, give plenty of notice and stay close to the business. But instead of doing mischief, they make positive continuing contributions—as mentors to their successor(s), and as the "elder statesmen" to key customers, suppliers and industry contacts.

Did one of those descriptions hit home? The closer the founder can come to the Ambassador's departure style, the more graceful the exit and the more effective the Founder's Transition.

### Element #4: Financial Independence

It may seem a bit bizarre to be stressing the importance of financial independence to someone who owns a successful family business. But many business owners who have ample net worth on paper still depend on their business for most of their income stream and asset base. This presents the following challenge:

> *If you will be dependent on the business for your income and asset strength in retirement, you will never really let go!*

It makes no difference how much you think you trust your successors. In most cases this trust is not complete enough for you to be comfortable depending on them for your financial well-being. From an income standpoint, you want and deserve a comfortable lifestyle after all those years of sacrifice. If the only income-producing asset you own is the business, can it realistically afford to continue to pay your salary in addition to that of the new top executive?

From the standpoint of your asset base, is your investment portfolio so heavily weighted toward your business that it is out of balance? Those income and asset conditions describe the situations of far too many founders and leaders today. If this describes your current situation, begin to develop tactics for diversifying your asset base and for developing sources of retirement income that are independent of the business.

### Keep Your Sense of Humor

We have described the most essential elements of the Founder s Transition. Having established the importance of this transition, we are almost ready to turn our attention to the second of the Six Transitions in our balanced succession planning model—the Family Transition. Before we move on, there is at least one other potential roadblock—your frame of mind.

We have worked with family businesses long enough to have heard numerous reasons why founders "can't" let go. There are definite trends in founders' thinking on this subject, and because there seem to be "top 1O'Tists for everything else in our culture, here is our list of "The Top 10 Reasons Founders Can't Let Go":

**Reason #10:** *"Too many people I've known have died (or acted dead) soon after they retired."* While there are indeed studies that report a direct correlation between mortality and retirement, the antidote is to follow other passions. The real danger is idleness. Avoid the "couch potato syndrome."

*Reason #9: "Without mey the business is nothing."* A more accurate statement might be, "Without me there would have been no business." Successful businesses evolve. The founder will forever get credit for being the founder. But time passes and new demands may be placed on the business that require a different set of skills than those possessed by the founder.

**Reason #8:** *"Without the business, I'm a nothing."* The founder needs to establish an identity separate from the business, and this doesn't happen overnight. That is one reason to start planning the Founder's Transition well before the "due" date.

**Reason #7:** *"I hate gardening, get seasick on cruise ships and get sunburned if I play too much golf or tennis."* Many founders spend years saying there were so many things they wanted to do if only they had the time. Well, now you will have the time, so find that wish list. Think creatively. Your talents are needed somewhere in the community. Consider the universities. Nobody is ever too old to learn—or to teach. How about becoming an advisor to a start-up business? The possibilities are limited only by our imaginations.

**Reason #6:** *"I need somewhere to go every day."* Has your spouse mentioned that you married for better or for worse, but not for lunch every day? Major changes such as retirement can add new stresses to any relationship. What do you think your spouse has been doing while you were fully occupied in the business? You both had a routine for years. In fact, your spouse's routine was probably not very dependent on you. Well, yours may be changing, but that does not mean your spouse wants his or her routine to change as drastically. To help avoid postretirement stress in your family relationships, reread reasons 10, 8 and 7.

**Reason #5:** *"The kids want to change the way the business is run. If I'm not there, they will change what I've built"* In today's highly competitive, rapidly changing business environment, a business that doesn't change to keep up with new demands will find itself obsolete. Under your leadership the business has changed from the day of its founding. Why should it stop now? Change is constant and your business will thrive on an infusion of fresh ideas and energy.

**Reason #4:** *"I need a successor but don't want to choose between my kids."* If you think the choice is hard when you are around, it will become a much more complicated one after you're gone. You could die in the saddle and let them "duke it out," but the business could be "KO'd" in the process. It is healthier for both the business and the family to establish the pattern of succession with the founder still involved.

**Reason #3:** *"The business is my income source. I have to stay active to protect my cashflow."* There are a vast array of strategies for develop ing retirement income sources that are independent of the business. It is better for both you and the business if you select and implement one or two of them. Seek the counsel of a competent professional financial advisor.

**Reason #2:** *"Nobody can run the business as well as I can."* You may not realize it, but you're probably not the only one running the business now. You may make the major decisions, but you are probably not involved in all the details. Step back! Look around! You may find untapped potential.

**Reason #1:** *"They may run it better than I did."* If they do, you've just hit the jackpot. When this really happens, then you have successfully negotiated the twists and turns of the Founder's Transition. Enjoy your retirement knowing your business is growing in value under capable leadership.
Congratulations!

## A Word to the Next Generation

We believe the founder's story should be visible in the family business today. It reinforces the sense of history, purpose and vision that are so often diluted as time slips by. Do you know the founder's story? If not, learn it. Document it. Make it a part of corporate lore so that all succeeding generations and employees will know it well. Do your children know it? If not, tell them!

*"'There is no use trying,' said Alice.*
*'One can't believe impossible things.'*
*'I dare say you haven't much practice,' said the Queen.*
*'When I was your age,*
*I always did it for half-an-hour a day.*
*Why, sometimes I've believed as many as*
*six impossible things before breakfast.'"*

LEWIS CARROLL
*Alice's Adventures in Wonderland*
1865

## CHAPTER TWO

### *The Family Transition*

The Family Transition is the second enabling transition. As with the Founder's Transition, the influence of the Family Transition is felt throughout all four of the implementation transitions. Perhaps the best way to get perspective on the Family Transition is to recall the mental image of your family on top of the triangle. With that in mind, consider the following:

> **The Goal of the Family Transition**
> *To make your family's movements in search of balance purposeful rather than random!*

It is in the Family Transition that the trade-offs between business prosperity, family harmony and personal well-being are met head-on. This direct confrontation makes the Family Transition, without a doubt, the most challenging of the six succession transitions.

In dealing with each transition we have isolated the key elements most critical to that transition. Thus, here are the five critical elements of a successful Family Transition.

#1. Understanding the impact of the difference between family values and business values

#2. Adopting the "and/both" perspective of family/business decisions and discarding the "either/or" philosophy

#3. Managing your hat collection, i.e., recognizing the rights and responsibilities that accompany the various roles in which family members can find themselves

#4. Understanding your family myths—the unspoken "laws" that affect the behavior of everyone in the family

#5. Learning and practicing effective communication skills that all families need but few families have really learned

### Element #1: Value Differences

Virtually every book written about family businesses will contain at least one chapter concerning the conflict between business values and family values. In some cases, that subject is the entire book!

Obviously this is an important topic. It is generally accepted that the existence of conflicting value systems is what distinguishes family businesses from nonfamily businesses. If that is true, then dealing effectively with the reality of conflicting values is central to the notion of family business success.

We agree that this is a core concept, but from our perspective it is but one of several key components of the family business transition. Understanding that family and business values differ is important, but in a vacuum such understanding is virtually worthless. The resolution of these value differences must be handled within the context of the other four components of the Family Transition.

The starting point is to identify the relationship between family values and business values. To illustrate this concept, we want to acquaint you with nine primary value differences that present the greatest challenge to the majority of our clients.

### 1. Emotion/Objectivity

**Families** are, generally, emotionally based systems. Decisions are most often made on the basis of feelings rather than objective criteria.**Businesses** are more objectively based.While there is a place foremotion in business, objective decision-making is the norm.

### 2. Membership Terms

**Families** offer lifetime membership. We are born into our families and our membership card bears no expiration date. No matter how much physical and emotional distance you try to put between you and your relatives, you will always be part of your family. **Businesses** have earned memberships. An individual is hired into a business because he or she possesses a set of skills and abilities that the business needs. When an employee is terminated from a business, the business membership is canceled.

### 3. Relations/Results

**Families** are driven by relationships. It makes good sense. If we re in it for life and there are no skill requirements, then what we take to the bank in the family setting are harmonious, satisfying relationships.

**Businesses** are driven by results. This also makes sense. A business must take money to the bank. That means the people in the business must produce results with tangible value—day after day, month after month, year in and year out. And if they don't? Well, remember the business value concerning membership.

## 4. Unity/Competition

**Families** thrive when there is unity among all members. It represents a unique source of support. In reality, competition does exist in families, and can be seen in "sibling rivalry." However, these behaviors are viewed as problematic—something families work to reduce. Additionally, those who are dissenters in families stand out. They are the proverbial "black sheep." But even they, like the prodigal son, can look to the family when the chips are down.

**Businesses** thrive on competition. And because a business demands results from its people, there is internal competition as well. Those who deliver the best results most consistently will fare better than the rest. Individuals with new and different ideas are sought after and valued for the new challenges they bring into the company.

## 5. Security/Risk

**Families** are like safety nets. They like and trust what is familiar. Family members are protective of one another. Most families are reluctant to let one of their own fall too far, and will work to cushion the landing. Because they thrive on unity and support, they provide family members with a sense of security and try to eliminate risk.

**Businesses** and risk go hand in hand. They are investments in which the reward is proportionate to the risks taken. Businesses have to be willing to accept prudent risks, and individuals who work in businesses must be risk takers.

## 6. Equality/Equitability

**Families** place a strong emphasis on equality. Parents try to give their children equal time. Gifts should be of equal value. Estate plans are typically designed so that heirs share equally in their parents' wealth. "Fair" and "equal" are synonymous in families.

**Businesses** operate on the principle of equitability. In the business world, "fair" and "equal" are not synonyms. To be equitable, it is necessary for businesses to differentiate based on individual contributions. If businesses followed the principle of equality rather than equitability, then the newest hire on the production floor and the president would have the same pay rate.

## 7. Avoidance/Confrontation

**Families** learn to sidestep the tough issues that they believe will be emotionally "messy." After all, family relationships are based on unity and support, and family members want life to be as smooth as possible. Confronting a difficult issue involving a family member may cause hurt feelings. If we're not sure how to close the wound, the most comfortable course of action may be to not open it in the first place. This is why developing effective communication skills is so important to family health.

**Businesses,** of necessity, must confront tough issues. Failure to do so will contribute to business failure. So, as a business leader, we take a deep breath and tackle that which is difficult and unpleasant because we have no choice.

## 8. Directed Inward/Looking Outward

**Families** are insular. In order to be a source of safety and security, families erect and maintain an invisible but impermeable shield that protects family members from unwanted intrusions by outsiders.

**Businesses** are outwardly directed. Any business must be constantly interacting with the external environment. If not, it loses touch with its customers, competitors and suppliers and it will quickly find itself at a disadvantage.

## 9. Status Quo/Change

**Families** work hard to preserve the status quo because it provides a sense of security. Families feel more comfortable when familiar patterns are repeated. An often overlooked consequence of such major family events as births, deaths, marriages and divorces is that they stimulate changes in the family's routine.

**Businesses** find it unacceptable to merely maintain the status quo. Successful businesses are constantly changing to keep up with or stay one step ahead of the needs of their various constituents. For executives and managers, part of being successful in business means taking on the mantle of "Change Master" and wearing it well.

## Element #2: "And/Both" Instead of "Either/Or"

There is one other way in which our perspective on the values conflict is different.

> *Lasting resolution of the conflict between family values and business values lies in replacing traditional "either/or" thinking with the "and/both" perspective.*

On the next page we've documented traditional "family first" and "business first" approaches to applying family and business values to three typical family business questions. Put your "Boss" hat on for a moment. You will probably find that it is easy to choose the answers from the business column.

## Traditional "Either/Or" Thinking

| FAMILY BUSINESS QUESTIONS | "FAMILY FIRST" ANSWERS | "BUSINESS FIRST" ANSWERS |
|---|---|---|
| How do we make decisions about hiring family members? | Hire any relative who needs a job, whether or not there is an opening. | Select the best candidate—either family or nonfamily, and only when there is an opening. |
| How do we compensate family members? | Pay them all the same and either:<br>(A) Expect them to work for "peanuts" because it is their duty to the family.<br>or<br>(B) Pay them more than they are worth to assure a desired lifestyle. | Pay within competitive ranges. Let performance determine position within the range. Differentiate based on the inherent value of the job and performance of the individual. |
| How do we deal with performance issues involving family members? | Avoid performance reviews and penalties for substandard performance. It may cause hurt feelings (and nonfamily supervisors are reluctant to evaluate family members). | Mandate that supervisors provide performance reviews to all employees and take appropriate action to respond to all performance problems, including dismissal. |

Now think like both a "boss" and a "parent." You will likely find that the choices get a bit tougher. If you can't make the choice, you're not alone. In practice, selecting between only the "family first" or "business first" options can immobilize many a "boss/parent."

We know you have been (and will continue to be) faced with such questions. The overlap between the two value systems is a well-known fact. It comes with the territory and is part of every family business. That relationship is depicted graphically below.

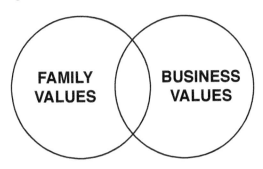

Finding themselves firmly impaled upon the sharp horns of such dilemmas, most family business executives feel that they are in what appears to be a lose/lose situation. Indeed, if they must make an "either/or" decision, there is no good answer. In most family businesses, making a decision that puts the business first and ignores the needs of the family means having to face the family consequences. Exclusive "business only" decisions threaten family harmony.

Similarly, making a decision that keeps family consequences at a minimum usually means paying a price in terms of business considerations. Too many "family only" decisions threaten business prosperity. It's an uncomfortable position in which to find oneself. The response is predictable. Decision paralysis sets in. With the decision makers immobilized, the emotional power of the family values will eventually prevail:

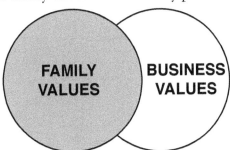

It is like a growing eclipse. Over time the family values will become so prevalent in the business that they will overshadow and begin to displace the business values. As the process continues, family values will displace too many business values, and both the business and the family will suffer.

The tragedy is that what seems like a weakness is really an asset. When it is understood and well managed, this interplay between family and business values becomes a source of strength for family businesses. All those positive, powerful attributes listed on page 16 in the Executive Briefing are driven by the overlap of the two value systems.

Every family business has a choice. It can make the inescapable interaction of its two primary value systems a source of conflict or a source of strength. And every family member has the power to move the family business system in either direction. We presume that anyone reading this book will opt for strength over conflict. Moreover, we presume that they will work actively on behalf of family business strength if they have the right tools. The two basic tools in your kit are **perspective and knowledge**.

The **perspective** you need is that the two value systems are in conflict—and always will be. Given that reality, there is a serious problem with applying "either/or" thinking in your decision making. This kind of thinking does nothing more than heighten the tension between two value systems that are already at odds.

Remember the principle of **Family and Business—both in balance**. The natural result of forced choices between either the family system or the business system is that one system is disregarded. And when one system is totally disregarded, both systems lose!

It may help to visualize a balance beam (much like a see-saw) with the family on one end and the business on the other. You achieve balance by where you elect to place the fulcrum. "Either/or" decisions force you to place the fulcrum at either the family end of the see-saw:

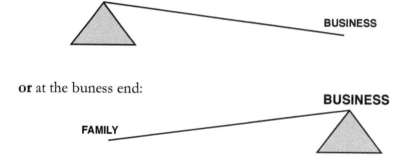

**or** at the buness end:

It really doesn't matter which end you choose. It is physically impossible to achieve balance by placing the fulcrum too close to either end.

The **knowledge** you need is that a third set of choices exists if you take the "and/both" approach. For "and/both" decisions the fulcrum is carefully adjusted between the two ends of the balance beam. The degree of adjustment depends on what your family decides together about which decision criteria to use.

Suppose the issue is principally a business decision, but it does have family consequences. In this situation it is best to consider decision alternatives that respect both family and business considerations but give preference to the business aspects.

On the other hand, you may be making what is primarily a family decision but with consequences for the business. Under these circumstances, consider decision options that give preference to the family aspects without completely disregarding business considerations.

Balancing your decision making may seem to be a tough order to fill, but not if you collaborate creatively to identify options. Examples of the same three questions to which we previously applied "either/or" answers are provided in the table on page 50, only this time we have suggested "and/both" answers.

We've provided only one sample "and/both" answer to each question. Moreover, our examples may not be the right "and/both" decisions for your family business. There are other "and/both" options. The challenges are:

- To think "outside the box"
- To work cooperatively in the effort

Getting to "and/both" answers is not always easy. The job will be even harder if you try to get there alone. And once you've made the decision yourself, you will still need to "sell" it to everyone else. We recommend using family council meetings and family retreats to share the effort. (Refer to part III, "Practical Tools")

| FAMILY BUSINESS QUESTIONS | "AND BOTH" ANSWERS |
| --- | --- |
| How do we make decisions about hiring family members? | When there is an opening, we will give preference to qualified family members with experience outside the family business. |
| How do we compensate family members? | We will apply all prevailing compensation policies, and will add a 5% wage/ salary premium for family- member employees. |
| How do we deal with performance issues involving family members? | Family-member employees will receive performance reviews given jointly by their immediate supervisor and a family- member manager. The family business will be more willing to fund additional educational and training experiences to develop the competency of family members. |

The story of the two hats we recounted in the beginning of the book provides an opportunity to apply "and/both" thinking. Try building your own balanced "and/both" epilogue to the story. Imagine you have just fired an underperforming son or daughter in your own family business. What follows?

Anger? Perhaps. At the very least, your child wouldn't be happy about what happened.

Embarrassment? Probably. You can be reasonably sure that no one in his or her circle of friends has been fired by their father or mother.

A door forever closed? Only if you shut it.

Opportunity? There can be tremendous opportunity with "and/both" thinking. Suppose that rather than creating a purely punitive experience, you provide outplacement counseling or use your business contacts to help find him or her a job outside the business. Imagine leaving the door open to consider a return to the family business. The only conditions would be that he or she has gained perspective, built confidence, demonstrated competence, tasted real accomplishment and developed personal discipline elsewhere. (This assumes, of course, that he or she is still interested in the family business and there is an appropriate opening). Finally, imag ine that person returning with self-esteem, skills and knowledge that add value to the business and help build the bottom line.

If you can imagine creative solutions such as this, then you are well on your way to mastering the art of "and/both" thinking.

## Element #3: Hats OfF to You!

The third element of the Family Transition concerns multiple roles and managing the boundaries between these roles. Many hats are available to everyone in a family business and managing your hat collection becomes the responsibility of each family member.

To avoid overcomplicating an already difficult transition, we'll limit ourselves to the 15 primary hats. Other possibilities exist, but first master managing the most obvious hats. In no implied order of priority, they are: (1) Founder; (2) Owner; (3) Chief Executive; (4) Manager; (5) Nonmanagement Employee; (6) Director; (7) Dad; (8) Mom; (9) Spouse; (10) Son or Daughter; (11) Sibling; (12) In-law; (13) Aunt; (14) Uncle; and (15) Cousin.

## Business Hats: Rights, Responsibilities and Accountability

Managing so many hats is always a challenge. But the challenge becomes more reasonable if the family shares an understanding of the rights, responsibilities and accountability that come with each hat. It will facilitate the Family Transition if you and your family can agree on the attributes of each business hat.

Our specifications serve as a starting point. Your family may add additional attributes to fit your unique situation. It is important that everyone in the family understands and agrees with the model.

**Founder:** If you own the Founder hat, you have the right to do just about anything you want. There is only one of those hats in each business, and it only fits on the founder's head. The responsibility that goes with the Founder hat is to take the lead in the succession-planning process. This means ensuring the best future for the business, whatever form that future may take.

**Owner:** If you have an Owner hat in your collection, you have three basic rights: (1) to elect directors (who have a fiduciary responsibility for protecting the best interest of all owners); (2) to vote on "major" decisions reserved for owners in the bylaws; and (3) to expect a "fair" return on your investment. The responsibility that comes with this hat is to make reasoned, rational, informed decisions when exercising your rights. It is reasonable to expect an owner to vote his or her head and not with the heart. Owners are accountable to themselves and the other owners.

**Chief Executive Officer:** The CEO hat carries the responsibility for the overall performance of the business. If you possess this hat, you are the link between the board of directors and operating management, and you take the lead in crafting the strategic direction of the business. The chief executive typically has the right to select the top management team, and is accountable to the board for performance according to the standards it sets.

**Manager:** Managers are responsible for getting things done by leveraging themselves through others, and for meeting performance standards set between themselves and the CEO. Those who own a Manager hat have the right to expect fair treatment and equitable compensation in return for their competence and contribution to the business. Members of top management are accountable to the chief executive officer, while the subordinate managers are accountable to the appropriate member of top management. (Note: Although the parent may be the chief executive, that does not automatically make the child the parent s direct report.)

**Employee:** Owners of an Employee hat occupy nonmanagerial positions in the family business. They have the same rights as managers, and are responsible for direct completion of assigned tasks at or above standards established and agreed upon between the employee and his or her immediate supervisor, to whom the employee is accountable.

**Director:** If you possess a Director hat, you have been elected by the owners to be part of the governance arm of the business. You have accepted a fiduciary responsibility to protect the best interests of all the owners. (Note: If you are a director, it helps to know the definition of the term "best interests of all the owners.") Specific responsibilities should be spelled out in the bylaws of the business. Your accountability is to the owners. A director has the right to be fairly compensated for his or her services and to be indemnified against liability for other than irresponsible and/or illegal actions.

(More information about directors is available in John Ward's book *Creating Effective Boards for Private Enterprises.*

| BUSINESS HAT | RIGHTS | RESPONSIBILITY | ACCOUNTABILITY |
|---|---|---|---|
| FOUNDER | Virtually unlimited | Lead the succession-planning process | Self |
| OWNER | 1. Elect directors<br>2. Vote on matters specified in bylaws<br>3. Fair return | Make reasoned, informed decisions on ownership matters | Self and other owners. |
| CHIEF EXECUTIVE | 1. Fair treatment<br>2. Equitable compnesation per market/performance | 1. Overall business performance according to goals set by board<br>2. Lead development of strategic vision and plan | Board of directors |
| MANAGER | 1. Fair treatment<br>2. Equitable compensation per market/performance | 1. Performance of assigned function/business unit<br>2. Getting work done through others | Top management to chief excutive, funtional manager to immediate supervisor |
| EMPLOYEE | 1. Fair treatment<br>2. Equitable compensation per market/performance | Complete assigned taskds to established standards | Immediate supervisor |
| DIRECTOR | Equitable compensation | 1. Protect owner's interests<br>2. Hire chief executive<br>3. Strategic direction/policies | Owners |

> *To this point we have covered the six*
> *business-related hats. Notice that all*
> *accountability is to other business hats . . .*
> *not to any of the six family hats!*

## Family Hats: Roles and Responsibilities

In businesses we talk in terms of rights, responsibilities and account-ability. Families, however, do not operate like businesses. In families, the focus tends to be on roles and responsibilities, and not so much on rights or accountability. Specific family-based roles and responsibilities differ from family to family. However, each family hat has a stereotype attached to it, and those stereotypes are reasonably accurate in a general sense. Try these hats on for size.

**Dad**: The big role for owners of Dad hats is to provide models for their children. Sons look to Dad for clues to what it means to be a hus-band and a father. Daughters look to Dad to develop a sense of the roles the male plays in adult male-female relationships. Dads who own one or more business hats as well have a unique challenge. If you have learned how to wear the right hat for any occasion, that is the model your children will most likely adopt. If you have spent a lifetime wearing the wrong hat, or trying to wear two (or more) hats at once, your children will not learn how to make the appropriate distinctions. Your responsibilities (ones you share with Mom) are to nurture, guide, support and mentor your children; to enable them to become competent, balanced adults. These responsi-bilities will instill within them those values that provide the foundation from which responsible adults make positive contributions to the world in which they live.

**Mom**: If you have one of these hats in your collection, you play a vital role in family leadership. In many families, that person with the Dad hat may look like he has the power, but the proverbial "power behind the throne" rests with Mom. You are the unofficial clearinghouse for the complex interactions within the family. Whether or not you are the CEO (chief executive officer) of the family business, you are most probably the CEO (chief emotional officer) of the family. It is from Mom that daugh-ters learn the roles of wife and mother. In a growing number of families where Mom is also a business executive, she provides a model for juggling business and family roles at the same time. Sons look to Mom to pick up clues about appropriate adult male-female relationships. You share with your spouse the same responsibilities we discussed in the section on the Dad hat.

**Son or Daughter:** The Son or Daughter hat is heavy. You may not know it, but your parents see your role as being the hope for the future— the continuation of the family legacy. Your responsibility is to honor your parents. The lessons you learn in your family will last a lifetime. Patterns tend to repeat themselves. Therefore, if family dynamics have been positive, you will have a good foundation for the future. If they have been negative, you may need help weaving a new pattern.

**Siblings:** Those of us who have raised children might assume that siblings5 roles and responsibilities are to make life miserable for the other siblings in the family. In the 1930s, Alfred Adler suggested that roles varied with birth order. The firstborn child is the achiever, independent and a survivor; the second born is more relaxed and wily and the youngest is driven to succeed. Whether to "buy in" to Adler's theory is a matter of choice. Whatever their roles, the siblings' responsibility is to enhance their own self-esteem without destroying the other siblings or viewing them as rivals. Note to Mom and Dad hat wearers: You will play a large part in this. The family dynamics you foster will either facilitate or block your children's ability to differentiate themselves from their siblings in positive ways.

**In-laws:** We have fantasized about what shape and form an In-law hat might take. It would probably be some kind of "Rube Goldberg" contraption. When In-laws get their hat, it must be added to whatever hats they bring with them from their own families. For some, owning the in-law hat brings unlimited access to any and all business hats in their new family. For others, access is limited. For yet others, access is denied. There are rules of family behavior hidden inside the headband of the In-law hat, but they are illegible. The in-law may believe that the rules that come with his or her "old" family hats are better, and they may well be. But there is probably no safe way to express that belief. In short, if you wear an In-law hat, your role is to walk through a mine field. Your responsibility is to not step on any mines!

**Aunts and Uncles:** When more than one nuclear family is involved in a family business, the Aunt and Uncle hats come into play. The role of aunts and uncles is to provide similar modeling as the mother and father. A potential advantage that aunts and uncles have is that they can often be more effective mentors than can Mom and Dad. The emotional ties between aunts and uncles and their nieces and nephews are not quite as strong as the ties between parent and child. Thus, they can often promote more objectivity, which enhances their effectiveness as mentors.

**Cousins:** If there are aunts and uncles involved in the family business, then there will probably also be cousins. If that is the case, then cousins will likely become part of the next-generation management and ownership teams. Thus, building a cooperative relationship among cousins contributes significantly to the success of both the management and ownership transitions. Siblings raised by the same parents typically share a common orientation and value system. Because cousins are raised with different sets of parents, there may well be more than one value system brought into the next-generation management and ownership teams. These differences need to be identified, reconciled and accommodated.

Managing your hat collection is really an exercise in managing boundaries. The essential elements of good boundary management are:

1.  Knowing the roles, rights and responsibilities that go with each hat

2.  Knowing which hats you own and which you don't

3.  Wearing the right hat at the right time. (For example, if you are involved in an ownership decision, make it only with your Owner hat on. If it is a family decision, put your various business hats back in the drawer.)

4.  Not wearing a hat you don't own! In other words:

> *BEFORE ANY DECISION, MAKE A HAT CHECK!*
> *NO HAT . . . NO VOTE!*

### Element #4: Family Myths

Years ago when Ernie, who is not a psychologist, first heard the term "family myth," he recalled a phrase about "separating myth from reality." His immediate reaction was that a family myth must be something about a family that is not true. As it turns out, "myth" is a term that psychologists use to describe a set of beliefs that provide structure for the behavior of a society. "Family myths" are the beliefs that explain the behavior of a family.

In society in general, myths teach us how different social groups have answered basic questions about their world and an individuals place within that world. Studying a society's myths leads to perspective about how people developed a particular social system and the customs of that system.

Now focus on that segment of society we call a family. Better yet, focus on your own family. If you look closely enough, you can identify some of the family myths that govern its behavior. Those that we see repeatedly are:

- Conflict is to be avoided at all costs.
- Never say anything negative to Mom or Dad until after dinner.
- The eldest comes first.
- The baby needs protection.
- A woman's place is in the home.
- Equal treatment is above all else.
- What Dad says, goes.
- If you want to change Dad's mind, see Mom.
- Disagreement shows lack of respect.
- Stay "in step" with the majority, or become a "black sheep."
- Don't trust outsiders.
- Don't let in-laws get too close.

Here are two bits of perspective about family myths that will serve you well in your quest for balance.

### 1. We can't always recite them, but we know what they are.

Have you ever tried to give someone directions to a place to which you have gone hundreds of times? You could get there with your eyes shut, but you can't remember the name of one street at which you make a left turn. Well, that's the way it is with family myths. We have lived with them all our lives, so we just know what they are but often have trouble articulating them.

### 2. In-laws have to learn the hard way.

Big sister gets married. Happy day! Everyone welcomes their new brother-in-law into the family. Hugs! Kisses! Handshakes! Enthusiastic assurances of eager acceptance! But nobody tells him the family myths. He never gets a copy of the rule book because the rule book has not been written. In most families, these "rules" have never even been discussed. It gets worse. This newcomer grew up in his own family with its own set of family myths. You can be certain that the myths in his family are different than the myths in yours. Without a "rule book" in hand, the only way the new brother-in-law is going to learn your family's rules is by breaking them! Be assured that if you walk through a mine field long enough without a map, you are going to step on a mine. He will. And if he steps on too many, the in-law becomes "the outlaw."

On the other hand, in-laws often have a much more objective perspective of their new family. They can see when the proverbial emperor is naked, and are often the most honest reporters of the family's mythology

> **What are your family's myths?**

## Element #5: Learning and Applying Communication Skills

Communication is one of our most critical life skills. The degree to which you develop successful communication skills has a significant impact on the quality of your personal and professional lives. It is the "emotional glue" that creates healthy, positive relationships.

Families communicate. When children are young and everyone is at home, families communicate daily. As the children grow into adulthood and create their own lives, communication may become less frequent, but it is still occurring. Communicating is not the issue. Communicating effectively is the challenge. This is one of the most problematic areas with which we deal when we consult with family businesses.

### Special Communication Challenges for Family Businesses

Communication is important for all families. However, without involvement in the family business, many adult children move away from their families of origin. When they do, the frequency of communication with family members decreases. Under these conditions, the lack of effective communication skills may be somewhat more tolerable because family interaction is limited and primarily social. This is not the case in family businesses where adults not only socialize but work together and confront business problems together virtually every day. When these same adults lack effective communication skills, problems often go unsolved and become magnified. This can negatively impact business prosperity, family harmony and personal well-being.

### It Sounds Easy Enough

The dictionary definition of communication is "a giving or receiving of information." This definition is deceptively simple. Why, then, is it so difficult in so many family businesses? Families rarely take the time to understand the complexities of the communication process, or to learn the techniques of effective communication. Families just talk, often with insufficient regard for what is said or how the words come out.

In our prior discussion of family and business values regarding avoidance and confrontation, we pointed out that families try to avoid confrontation. This does not mean that there may not be significant confrontation in many families. But the natural tendency is to back away from discussing any issue that could raise the emotional temperature. As a result, two kinds of issues exist within any family—those that can be easily discussed and those that are known to exist but are relegated to the "unspoken" category.

Unfortunately, not talking doesn't solve the problems. They don't go away. They simply stay under the surface and fester. They build in intensity until they finally surface in an uncontrolled eruption. Pent-up anger, frustration and resentment do not lead to reasonable dialogue.

### Family Myths and Communication

Earlier we talked about "family myths" as the unwritten rules that guide family behavior. Some of these myths that directly affect communication in a family include:

- Be careful what you say to Mom or Dad or they will get angry and upset.
- Avoid sensitive or controversial subjects.
- To disagree is to show disrespect to elders.
- Nice people don't get angry.
- We don't argue with people we love.
- The person who yells the loudest and longest, wins.

Myths such as these lead to avoidance of issues and to the dysfunctional communication often experienced in family businesses.

### It Helps to Have a Flashlight

The communication challenge in family businesses much like a theme that we saw repeated many times in the now discontinued Calvin and Hobbes cartoon strip. If you have never seen it, Calvin is a little boy and Hobbes is his toy tiger. Hobbes is an inanimate stuffed animal in the company of adults, but very much alive when he and Calvin are alone. The theme is simple. Calvin and Hobbes are in bed with the lights out. Calvin is sure there is a monster under the bed. The more he thinks about the monster, the more gruesome it becomes. Finally, Hobbes shines a flashlight under the bed and the "monster" turns out to be a shoe (or some other similarly harmless object).

Many family communication rules leave family members in Calvin s spot. The lights are out and the "monster" is growing. Without good communication habits, they are ill equipped to deal with each other as adults in a business setting, and they can't find a flashlight.

> **If you want balance in your family business,
> you need a flashlight!**

### Breaking Bad Habits

Three processes—education, practice and structure—can markedly improve family communication.

**1. Education:** Many excellent programs are available that help individuals and groups learn more effective methods of communication. It is an extremely wise investment for family businesses to seek out such training.

**2. Practice what you learn:** Learning the techniques is only part of the challenge. Finally, it is necessary to put this training into practice. Use regularly scheduled family meetings and annual family retreats to practice communication skills. (See Practical Tool #7 for information on setting up these activities.) At the beginning it may be wise to retain a qualified professional to facilitate communication at family meetings and retreats. In the longer term, however, the family's ultimate goal should be to prepare themselves to assume the leadership of continuing meetings.

**3. Build models for resolving conflict and solving problems:** Families that adopt a systematic approach to problem solving and conflict resolution will realize greater benefit from applying the techniques of effective communication. The DoudHausnerVistar models for conflict resolution and problem solving are provided in part 3, the "Practical Tools" portion of this book.

You now have perspective about the two enabling transitions—the Founder's and the Family. Keep that perspective as you tackle the four implementation transitions.

*"'Would you tell me, please,
which way I ought to go from here?'
'That depends a good deal
on where you want to get to,' said the Cat.
'I don't much care where,' said Alice.
'Then it doesn't much matter
which way you go,' said the Cat."*

LEWIS CARROLL
*Alice's Adventures in Wonderland*
1865

## CHAPTER THREE

### *The Business Transition*

The quest for prosperity, harmony, well-being and balance is like a journey into uncharted territory. You need to make your own maps. Before you start drawing the maps, select some landmarks for reference points. Because the business is the greatest resource we have with which to create prosperity, it is an odds-on favorite to be one of our most important landmarks. That is why the Business Transition is part of the succession-planning process, and why it comes so early in the process.

The four key elements needed to get a true perspective of the Business Transition are:

#1. Understanding the business life cycle

#2. Developing effective and efficient operations

#3. Crafting a strategic vision

#4. Making clear financial assumptions

**Element #1: The Business Life Cycle**

Every business goes through a life cycle. Many people have written about this concept, all with slightly different slants on the process. In our view, the business cycle is comprised of six phases. The DoudHausnerVistar version of the business life cycle is depicted graphically on the following page.

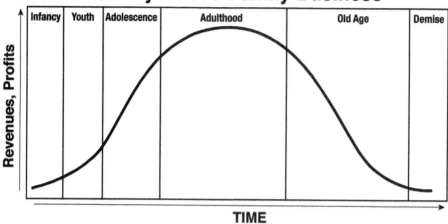

## Life Cycle of a Family Business

| Infancy | Youth | Adolescence | Adulthood | Old Age | Demise |

*Revenues, Profits* (vertical axis)

**TIME** (horizontal axis)

Anyone who has taken a basic marketing course will probably recognize that our model for the family business life cycle is similar to a product life cycle. It is, and with good reason. Many family businesses are "one-trick ponies," in which all, or the great majority of, revenues and profits are attributable to one product or service.

The time it takes a business to move through the cycle will vary based on a variety of factors including:

- The nature of the products and/or services provided
- The customer base served
- Local, regional, national and, increasingly, global economics
- **And, most importantly, the quality and timeliness of leadership and management decisions and actions**

Understanding how family businesses typically behave at various points in this cycle will help you determine where your business fits. See if you can recognize your business in the descriptions that follow. It is worth the time to find out because how you approach the other three critical elements of the Business Transition will be influenced by where your business is in its life cycle.

### Phase 1: Infancy—The Getting-Started Years

In Chapter 1 we talked about the founder's roles, and suggested that one of his or her first roles was as the initiator. Any business starts as a bright idea in the founder's head. As the idea begins to take form, the product is designed, plans are made, capital is acquired, people are hired and customers are courted.

A small band of devoted risk-takers works tirelessly to make the dream a reality. Start-up businesses look and behave like this:

- The identity of the business is tied to the founder.
- There is barely enough capital.
- Cash flow is iffy; the employees and the business live from payday to payday.
- There is no formal organization, no job descriptions.
- Everyone pitches in and does whatever has to be done.
- Procedures are kept in people's heads.
- Management meetings are people yelling down the hall at each other while running to fight the fire du jour.
- There are no policy manuals; people simply do what needs doing.
- Some business information is on a crumpled slip of paper in the founder's back pocket; the rest in his or her head.

These are both frightening and exciting times. The founder's home may be mortgaged to the hilt. The employees who are there at the start give up job security to be part of the adventure. If "the dream" doesn't come true, everyone loses time and money.

## Phase 2: Youth—The Growth Years

The next step in the business life cycle is the growth stage. The start-up risk paid off. More customers are buying more products. Some things change for the business in the early part of its growth period:

- Cash flow becomes more predictable, so you start looking weeks ahead rather than merely days.
- Bankers start to come calling because the business now has a successful track record.
- Suppliers are easier to deal with for the same reason.
- Black ink begins to show up on the bottom line.

But some things don't change very much at all:

- The founder's identity is still the organization's identity.
- Organization structure and management style are both still loose and informal.
- Reliable, timely information is hard to come by.

Later in the growth phase, still more changes occur. Financially, you will know you are there when:

- Sales are growing and the rate of sales growth is increasing.
- You are able to purchase raw materials more cost efficiently.
- Profitable months, quarters and years are now the rule rather than the exception.
- You are servicing your start-up debt with relative ease.

However, in the midst of all this prosperity, some small cracks are beginning to form:

- More people are hired and the organization becomes more complicated.
- You no longer know all your employees by name.
- The key people who used to see each other all the time are harder to reach.
- When they do get together, they argue (something they never used to do.)
- More people need more data; that crumpled piece of paper in the founder's back pocket and all the information stored in people's heads isn't good enough and, in fact, can expose the business to liabilities.

It is still a great time for the business, but in many little ways it just isn't as much fun as it used to be.

## Phase 3: Adolescence—The Coming-of-Age Years

At this point in its life cycle, it is time for the business to decide what it wants to be when it grows up. Any business has two basic choices: to mature into responsible adulthood, or to remain a perennial "teenager."

It isn't an easy choice. Most founders thrive on the informality and excitement that was part of the business's infancy and youth. They hate the thought of too much structure. It all sounds so rigid, so much like what they were trying to avoid when they started the business. You know your business is entering adolescence when you start wrestling with these alternatives.

The problems that began to surface late in the growth phase weigh on everyone's mind. Yet hope springs eternal. Maybe these problems are the adolescent business's version of pimples. We could decide to simply learn to live with them on the premise that they will all go away as we get older. But probably not.

All businesses have to work through this difficult time in their life cycles. Growing up is hard work. The benefit is that there are more rewards to be had in maturity. The risk of being a perennial teenager is that sooner or later the business will go into its declining years without ever reaping the benefits of mature adulthood.

Let us assume you choose to do what it takes to professionalize the business. The next question is "How?" Discovering "how" depends on your willingness to explore and find answers to two questions:

- Is the business operationally fit? (In other words, are we being efficient as managers?)
- Is the business strategically well positioned for the long term? (Are we being effective as leaders?)

We will more fully address these questions after we complete our life cycle tour.

## Phase 4: Adulthood—Years of Stability

One of the pleasant things about early adulthood is that it can be a time to enjoy the benefits of the hard work and sacrifice that went into growing up. During the early years of this phase, you will notice that the business is running smoothly and profitably. You've ironed out most of the kinks and have found a proven formula that works! But some subtle changes are taking place. In a maturing business:

- Sales are still growing, but if you look closely you'll find that the rate of growth is falling off.
- The business is profitable, but profits aren't increasing as fast as they once did, and margins are shrinking.

When you look for the causes of the shrinking margins, you find that one or more of the following is happening:

- You have more competitors than before.
- Your competitors can produce their products and services at a lower cost.
- Substitutes for your product have come to market.
- Customer needs and preferences are changing.
- Technological advances have made your product less attractive.

But the changes may be too subtle for anyone to notice. Or, more likely, the results are still too good for anyone to care.

Something else happens during early maturity. (Actually, it may have started way back in the later stages of the growth phase.) There is a natural and understandable tendency to start "harvesting" the excess cash generated by a successful business. Harvesting can do great things for your personal lifestyle. But before you start excessive indulgences, remember that rainy day. Cash reserves are necessary to make strategic investments that will ensure longer-term business health.

As the business moves further into the maturity phase, some less subtle changes take place. Look at this as the business equivalent of the sore joints and loss of energy the human body experiences as it ages:

- Sales growth levels off, or even starts to decline slightly.
- Last quarter's financials show the first red ink on the bottom line that has been seen since early in the growth phase.
- The shock may be eased somewhat when black ink reappears at the end of the next quarter.

Okay, we feel a little sore today. But the soreness goes away tomorrow. We're still fine. It was all just a momentary "blip."

## Phase 5: Old Age—The Declining Years

Personally we know we've entered this phase when that soreness doesn't go away the next day. In a business, the momentary blip isn't momentary anymore when:

- Sales are now declining because fewer customers buy fewer products or services.
- Cash flow deteriorates and turns negative.
- Your suppliers are tightening trade credit.
- Your best salespeople leave for greener pastures.
- Your production executive reminds you that the equipment isn't getting any newer, is breaking down more frequently and needs to be replaced.
- You would be glad to use some of your capital to upgrade the production equipment, but you can't because your cash is being pumped into operations to offset the negative cash flow.
- You decide you will have to borrow to make needed improvements, but the bankers (the ones who were courting you when times were good) are not returning your calls.
- Next comes the toughest call of all as you start laying off employees— including some really good people who have been with you for years.

Not a very pretty picture. These are trying times. Just ask anyone who has been there. Short of a minor miracle, the next person you call is either a turnaround specialist or a bankruptcy attorney.

### Phase 6: Demise—The Last'Years

It would be wonderful if we could omit this phase of the business life cycle. The reality, however, is that if you find yourself in decline, the end of the business is probably near. The bright side is that it really doesn't have to come to this.

The demise of virtually any business can be avoided if owners and managers will recognize the importance of change. Think again about Brien's Second Law of Business that we introduced in the Founder's Transition. **Sooner of later, the ability of any business to survive in spite of itself runs out!**

### Element #2: Operating Effectiveness and Efficiency

Looking for a break in the gloom and doom of Old Age and Decline? Well, you've come to the right place. As mortal human beings our life cycle must go from start to finish—which is why the Ownership and Estate Transitions are part of the balanced succession planning model. Businesses are more fortunate. They don't have to die.

In fact, the life of almost any business can be extended by the application of large doses of effective leadership and efficient management.

- Effective leadership is making timely choices to do the right things.
- Efficient management is having the competence to do the right things right.

We've known many effective leaders and efficient managers. They all apply four critical concepts that enable them to avoid the decline stage of the business fife cycle.

- Eliminate split business personalities.
- Embrace "professionalization."
- Keep the business physically and fiscally fit.
- Maintain perspective.

### Eliminate Split Business Personalities

Many of our clients demonstrate the following characteristics:
- Financially, the business is in the late stages of maturity—slowing growth, eroding margins, declining cash flow, etc.

- Organizationally, the business is still in its youth: There are no job descriptions, few (if any) performance standards, employees are starved for management information, etc.
- In terms of management style, the ever entrepreneurial founder/leader behaves as though the business is still in its infancy.

Wherever the business is in its life cycle, it won't survive and prosper with a split personality. The business—your business, our business, any business—needs to know where it is in the business life cycle and respond appropriately. Where is your business in the life cycle?

### Embrace "Professionalization"

Sooner or later every business needs to grow up and make the transition from youth to adolescence. We call that the process of "professionalizing" the ways in which the business is managed. We know that management systems and procedures must evolve to meet the changing needs of a growing business. Professionalization is an inevitable component of the success equation.

We also know that many entrepreneurial founders and leaders either dig in their heels or turn and run the other direction at the very mention of professionalizing the ways in which the business is managed. What you're left with is frustrated managers trying valiantly (but often hopelessly) to convince the person holding all the power that he or she should run the company differently—or at least allow them to run it more systematically and professionally.

### Keep the Business Physically and Fiscally Fit

Once you know where your business is in its life cycle, you can be an effective leader by deciding to do the right things. What are often called "growing pains" usually are signs that the business has become too complex for its existing management structure, staffing, policies, processes and procedures. The challenge is to allow your business to get into top shape for its age at any stage. Better yet, insist that it grow up and lead the charge. Take on the mantle of a Change Master and design a physical/ fiscal fitness program for your business.

Earlier in this chapter we suggested that two questions had to be addressed if the business was to move out of its youth, survive its adolescence and reap the benefits of adulthood. This concept addresses the first question: Is your business operationally fit?

Successful businesses are in top condition for their age, and they don't get that way by accident. A business needs a fitness program—a plan to get into shape and to stay in shape.

Designing a fitness program for your business really isn't difficult if you're smart about it. When a personal trainer designs an exercise program, he or she takes into account the subject's age, current physical condition and goals. The result is a balanced program that contains selected exercises, the right amount of weight or resistance, and a targeted level of exertion. Do the same thing for your business. Once you've decided where the weakest spots are, select the actions that fit your business—its age, its physical condition and its fiscal condition.

It makes no more sense to overstructure and oversystematize a start-up business in its infancy than it does to understructure and undersystematize a business that is moving rapidly through the growth of its youth and is in desperate need of help moving on to the next stage and coming of age. Similarly, a mature business may have all the people, professionalized systems and procedures it requires, but needs to get its products into shape and "tone up" capital equipment that is becoming obsolete.

When it comes to keeping your business in top shape, the first step is to evaluate its current condition. The Business Prosperity Profile, summarized on page 137, is a tool that will help you and your management team probe for possible trouble spots.

Obviously this isn't an all-inclusive list. We selected these 48 questions because it is these areas that cause most of the business problems experienced by the majority of our clients. Any question with a grade point average (GPA) of 2.5 or less is a likely candidate for inclusion in the fitness program you design for your business.

Remember, success is driven in large measure by knowing what to do.

### Maintain Perspective

You may have heard that in order to perpetuate success, the business has to be reinvented once in each product generation. That explains why software companies pour so much time and money into research and development. With an average product life of about 12 months, they must constantly reinvent themselves. The high attrition rate experienced in that industry simply proves that today's "hot" product is just that— today s, but not necessarily tomorrow's. The future is promised to no one. Effective leaders and efficient managers work hard at creating a future for their businesses.

Have you evaluated the useful lifespan of the products and services you provide right now? With this perspective you are able to recognize what many owners fail to understand: **The best time to invest in reinventing your business is during the good times when the uninformed believe that it is least necessary.**

### Element #3: Strategic Thinking

This is the third of the four key elements in the Business Transition. It addresses the importance of ensuring that your business is strategically well positioned for the long term.

It makes no difference whether your intent is to continue family ownership and management into the next generation, or whether you anticipate selling the business. Either way, the business will be stronger and more valuable if you become purposeful about identifying and acting on your strategic business vision.

### Practical Perspective on Strategic Vision and Strategic Planning

Consider that your business is on a continuous journey from where it is today to where it must be tomorrow. Planning is a part of any journey we take. And the longer and more complicated the journey, the greater the effort devoted to planning, the more detailed the plan and the greater the need for a travel guide.

Planning your business day is much like planning a cross-town drive. It is a relatively simple, informal process. Planning for the drive across town is merely a matter of thinking about the best route to the destination, and—if you live in a place like Los Angeles—the best time to leave. Planning your business day is simply a matter of knowing what must get done that day, and allocating the necessary time to accomplish your daily tasks.

Planning for the strategic future of your business is a different matter. An appropriate analogy would be planning a cross-country drive. That can require making decisions about how to best traverse unfamiliar territory. It may mean making decisions on matters about which you do not have complete knowledge. For example, the length of each day s segment can be planned, but you don't know for sure how good the roads will really be until you get on them. Hotel accommodations en route can be reserved in advance, but will the hotel really be as nice as it looked in the guidebook or on the Internet? Moreover, the overall success of the trip will involve matters over which you have no control—such things as weather conditions, and how heavy the traffic will be in the cities along the route.

When you decide to give up trying to plan alone and go to the auto club for help, they will start by asking the following questions:

- What is your point of departure?
- What is your destination?
- When do you need to arrive?

When the folks at the auto club have enough information, they will help you prepare your plan and document it. It is a long trip. Those strip maps and written reservation confirmations will come in handy.

Finally, all that planning is a waste of time unless you make sure your car is in good mechanical condition, and that you actually get in it, start driving, and keep going until you reach your destination.

Planning a cross-country trip is a good metaphor for strategic business planning because every factor involved in planning a long trip is involved in planning for the strategic future of your business:

- Knowing where you are.
- Understanding where you want to be.
- Deciding when you want to get there.
- Researching to acquire important information.
- Making important decisions about matters with which you are not entirely familiar, and accepting the fact that you can never get all of the information you would like to have.
- Considering the impact of factors beyond your control.
- Recognizing that planning works better when you include competent, knowledgeable people in the process rather than trying to do it alone.
- Getting the business in shape to support plan implementation.
- And, finally, having the will to actually implement the plan once it is developed.

In the conversation between Alice and the Cheshire Cat quoted at the beginning of this chapter, the cat showed Alice the importance of strategic vision. More recently, Yogi Berra became an advocate of strategic planning when he said, "If you don't know where you're going, you're liable to end up someplace else." Our proposition is that it very much matters that you know where you want to take your business and how you intend to get there.

The best way to do that is to:

- Have a vision for the future that all family members share.
- Translate that vision into a sense of mission for the business.
- Take a good, honest and structured look at your business and the outside environment that impacts the business.
- Define goals so that actual performance toward the goals will serve as indicators of progress.
- Determine what specific actions must be taken and what costs must be incurred in order to meet those goals.
- Assign responsibility for implementation and accountability for results.
- Track progress and make mid-course corrections as needed enroute.

The documented results of your efforts become the strategic plan for your business—your map for the journey.

Strategic planning is always hard work, but it does not have to be complicated work. A Fortune 500 company can employ a cadre of professional planners. They, in turn, will employ a variety of sophisticated modeling techniques to develop an impressive document. That is not what we are talking about here.

We advocate an approach to strategic planning that is better suited to the typical middle-market family business. It draws primarily on the accumulated knowledge of the leadership and management team.

There are two realities we find so prevalent in family businesses that we've reduced them to two rules about the reactions too many of these businesses have to the idea of strategic planning:

---

### Rule #1

*Common sense is no substitute for tradition!*

---

### Rule #2

*Indecision is the key to flexibility!*

---

The toughest part of strategic planning is that you must be willing to challenge virtually every assumption upon which you currently do business. In order to do that, you have to break both rules!

Are you prepared to break the rules? If so, then you are ready to draw a strategic map for your business, and provide the charts that will help managers and employees navigate the previously uncharted waters between today and tomorrow.

For the purposes of providing you with more perspective, here is a summary of the basic steps in the strategic planning process.

**Step 1.** Establish the family's vision for the business: Remember, this book is written for family-owned businesses. Unless the family possesses a shared vision for the future of its business, the effectiveness of the strategic plan will be seriously compromised. At the beginning of any family business, the strategic vision is typically set by the founder. In an interview with the founder of one of our client companies, he shared with us the vision that drove him to start his company and build it to $12 million in annual revenues. He said, "I wanted three things, and they were equally important to me. First, I wanted to make my dream of a new product a reality. Next, I wanted to be the master of my own destiny and to make a better living for my family than I could by working for someone else. The final part of my vision was to make the business part of my legacy to my family. I wanted this to be a place in which my son and daughter would want to work with me, and help me build a good business they would take over some day."

As clear and articulate about his vision as he was with us, he admitted he had never put it into words before, nor had he shared it with anyone else. Despite that, at the time we met him, his original product was a reality and others had been added to the mix. The business was a success, he was making a very good living, and his two children were working with him in the business. He had, for all intents and purposes, realized most of his vision. The operative question became, "What now?" Taking this to the next level meant bringing his wife and his son and daughter into the process of updating the vision so they would have a useful guide- post to support their decision making about the future.

**Step 2.** Build the planning team: Who should be the mapmakers? We advocate a participative approach to strategic planning. It may be the family's vision, but chances are good that you will depend on a group of people that includes non-family managers to move the business in the direction of that vision. They will be more committed to the journey if they help draw the map and the charts. As a general rule, the ideal size of a strategic planning team is 6 to 8 participants. Who are the 6 to 8 people in your organization most likely to influence the strategic direction of the business?

**Step 3.** Train the planning team: This step doesn't take very long. Just a couple of hours are all that is needed to brief the planning team on the process and their roles and responsibilities as participants.

**Step 4.** Gather planning data: The collective knowledge of the planning team, developed from years of experience, is a critical component of strategic planning and decision making. But intuition alone is not sufficient. Responsible strategic planning blends instinct with analysis of objective data. Therefore, when we facilitate strategic planning for a client, we gather hard data by taking the following actions:

- Administering and analyzing the results of the Business Prosperity Profile (see Practical Tool #1).
- Conducting interviews with each participant.
- Reviewing basic business documents.
- Determining additional data requirements and agreeing with top management on how data collection needs will be met.
- When necessary, overseeing data collection activities to ensure timely task completion.
- Once the data is collected, it needs to be compiled and distributed to the members of the planning team.

**Step 5.** Complete a strategic analysis: Recalling the comparison between strategic planning and trip planning, this step involves defining your point of departure. That means scanning both the internal and external environments using the data collected in Step 4. Each participant should conduct his/her own independent analysis of available data on the company, its competitors, the industry, and social and economic trends. That analysis should lead to conclusions about:

- Strengths and Limitations of the business (These are internal factors. Make conclusions about them based on your analysis of the results of the Business Prosperity Profile and analysis of financial, operating and organizational data.)
- Opportunities and Threats (These are external factors. Your analysis of data on competitors, suppliers, the industry and social/economic trends will help you draw conclusions about opportunities and threats.)

If you are using a facilitator to help guide you through the planning process, that individual or firm should complete the same exercise.

*(NOTE: Steps 6 through 10 are best done in a conference or retreat setting away from the business. Allow 2 ½ days.)*

**Step 6.** Review results of the strategic analysis: This step is taken to enable the members of the planning team to develop a unified focus on strategic issues. Because each individual will have completed his/her own individual strategic analysis, there will be some diversity of opinion about the conclusions that can be drawn from the data provided for that purpose. Allow each team member to present his/her conclusions. Next, provide time to discuss the similarities and differences. Finally, develop a consensus view of those strengths, limitations, opportunities and threats that should be addressed during the strategic planning process.

**Step 7.** Define the mission of the business: By completing Step 6, you will have defined the starting point—the first big step in the mapmaking exercise of strategic planning. The next task is to define the destination. The mission statement should be a clear and succinct statement of where you want the business to be in the future. Most vision statements are fairly general, and they should be. But mapmakers need to pinpoint their destination a bit more precisely. That is the purpose of a mission statement.

**Step 8.** Establish goals: Goals define in specific operational terms how success is supposed to look. We've defined our starting point with the strategic analysis. The vision statement provides a general idea about destination, and the mission statement has pinpointed it. Our strategic analysis has given us a general idea of some of the routes we can use to reach our destination. Before we select specific routes (see "Develop Strategies," below), we need the major milestones provided by our goals. Setting goals enable us to determine, in a general sense, whether we are on time and on course. For example, assume that one strategic goal is to double sales volume in the next three years. We'll follow this example in Step 9, below.

**Step 9.** Develop strategies: The strategies are our route map. They describe the major routes we intend to take to get the business past the major milestones established by our goals. Continuing the example started in Step 9, our strategies could include such items as:
- Developing and bringing to market 3 new products.
- Opening up sales territories in the Northwest.
- Creating and bringing on line export versions of selected products.

**Step 10.** Gear up for implementation: The time and effort invested in planning will be wasted without implementation. The actions to be taken to get ready to implement include:

- Assigning a champion for each strategy.
- Setting deadlines for action planning and budgeting (see Step 11).
- Examine what the organization needs to do very well in order to successfully implement the strategies.
- Consider how organization culture will impact implementation.
- Determine what needs to be done to align the organization and culture with these needs.

*(NOTE: Steps 11 and 12 are to be done immediately following the retreat).*

**Step 11.** Plan and budget for implementation: Strategy champions are responsible for going back into the organization and completing an implementation action plan and budget for the strategy (or strategies) for which they are responsible. Implementation cannot begin in earnest until the timing and need for finances and other resources have been identified.

**Step 12.** Make sure it can work: Test the feasibility of the plan so that all the owners can decide if the potential reward is worth the financial and investment risks.

**Step 13.** Communicate the plan: Once the plan has been approved by the owner(s), share your vision, goals, strategies and action plans with your employees. You need them to help you implement, so make sure they know what's ahead and how they fit in.

*(NOTE: Implementation should begin immediately. Steps 14 and 15 will be permanent parts of the implementation process).*

**Step 14.** Track progress: Don't take implementation for granted. Spend one day each quarter reviewing and evaluating progress. Not everything will go exactly as planned, so be prepared for the necessity of mid-course corrections and make them as needed.

**Step 15.** Celebrate successes: Be creative in finding ways to recognize and reward those at all organization levels who contribute to the many successes you will experience along the way.

**Step 1.** Do it all again: We do know how to count, and "Step 1" is not a misprint. It is simply our way of driving home the idea that strategic business planning is a never-ending process.

## Element #4: Financial Assumptions

From a financial perspective:

- Owners need to know what business results can be expected in order to make responsible ownership decisions, and
- Managers need to know what to expect from the owners in order to make responsible management decisions.

### For the Owners

In general terms, your family business will be either a growth-oriented investment, an income investment or some combination of these two.

Most owners theoretically understand these concepts. They are the basic foundations of investment decisions. In practice, however, few owners consider that distinction when they look at their own business.

One of the difficulties faced in many family businesses is that the owners have different investment objectives and different ways of defining the financial aspect of personal well being. Regardless of what your investment objectives may be, you'll be ahead of the game by knowing what you can expect financially from your business.

A start-up or growth business will probably consume all the cash it can get. If you own a piece of this kind of business and want meaningful distributions or dividends, you will be very disappointed.

The Adolescent business, one positioned between its Youth (the growth years) and Adulthood (a time of stability), may be able to both reinvest in itself and pay dividends. Or, in the case of an "S" corporation, the business may provide more cash than the minimum needed to pay taxes on reported distributions.

A more mature business may have less internal use for profits and, therefore, may pay even more in dividends or distributions.

But these are all generalizations. What should happen to the profits generated by your family business? Those of you who are on the board of directors are going to have to make that decision.

You have three basic choices: spend it on yourself, reinvest it in your business or invest it outside the business. The following guidelines will help you maintain the proper perspective as you consider your options:

- Spending it on yourself is understandable. Chances are you have sacrificed to get to this point and deserve some tangible rewards. You and your family deserve a good lifestyle. That is one of the dreams that got the business started in the first place. Remember, however, that your business deserves a good lifestyle as well.

- Reinvesting in the business is an important discipline. The business creates the resources that support your lifestyle of choice. If you take too much out, sooner or later the business will lose its ability to provide for you and your family. And never forget that the best time to reinvest in reinventing your business may be the time when it seems to need it the least. Why? Because resources are more readily available in good times, and the business will be better able to overcome the financial fallout of mistakes. However, there is another consideration. It is fairly easy to imagine business owners taking too much out of the business to spend on themselves. But we've met business owners who go too far in the other direction—leaving money in the business that could be used elsewhere more productively.
- Investing outside the business should be considered. Diversifying your asset base is an intelligent choice. No matter how attractive an investment your business may be, any responsible financial planner or investment advisor will verify the wisdom of a diversified portfolio. You may well want to use some of that discretionary cash to syndicate your risk and decrease your financial dependence on the business. (A side benefit of doing this is that it will facilitate a more effective Founder's Transition.)

While working on balancing prosperity, harmony and well being, be sure to use a balanced approach to determining financial priorities. Responsible directors and managers keep the owners informed about financial expectations.

## For the Business

We've established that one of the responsibilities of management and the board is to keep owners advised on what they can expect from the business financially. Now look at it from the other direction. One of the responsibilities of ownership is to keep the board and management advised of what the business can expect from the owners.

Individually, each owner has the right to want whatever he or she wants from an investment in the family business, including growth in value, generous dividends/distributions or a little of both. Collectively, however, there must be one unified message delivered to the business so that management can do its best to incorporate the owners' financial goals into the strategic business plan.

Finally, owners need to keep in mind that regardless of what they desire, the business may not be able to deliver it all the time. Mature businesses have reinvestment needs from time to time. Growth businesses do not always grow at a constant rate. Whatever the situation, twisting the business around (in effect, making it a contortionist) for the sake of the owners' personal financial desires is not very comfortable. If you must put the business in an uncomfortable position financially for the sake of the owners' needs, don't leave it there very long. You don't need a business with muscle cramps.

*"'If everybody minded their own business,'*
*said the Duchess in a hoarse growl,*
*'the world would go round*
*a deal faster than it does.'"*

LEWIS CARROLL
*Alice's Adventures in Wonderland*
1865

## CHAPTER FOUR

# *The Management Transition*

The operative question to be answered in the Management Transition is:

> ## *Who will run the business in the next generation?*

If your family business is facing a transition from the first generation to the second, you will have to create your first Management Transition plan. If you are moving from the second generation or beyond to the next, you have at least one example in place.

But don't rest on your laurels until you are sure that the last generation's Management Transition is a good example to follow. If you were there, you'll know firsthand. If you were not there, or were too young when it happened to remember, ask someone who was. Learn what worked well and went smoothly, and what difficulties occurred. Understand what mistakes were made, and what lessons should be learned as a result of the experience.

First-generation family businesses can use this chapter to develop a good Management Transition plan. Older family businesses can use it to test what they like and don't like about their past experiences.

A Management Transition is a big change in a family business. Many people have a great deal at stake. The founder's or current leader's graceful exit depends in part on this transition going well. The potential successors, who may have spent years jockeying for position in this race, have their futures on the fine. The rest of the family doesn't want war. And the other owners? The value of their ownership is at stake. With all that hanging in the balance, a smooth Management Transition pays off for everyone.

The three key elements to consider when building an effective Management Transition plan are:

#1. Recognizing that the current management model will and must change

#2. Clarifying options and opportunities

#3. Becoming serious about developing the next generation of leaders and managers

There are two important follow-up steps: making the decision and committing the plan to writing.

## Element #1: The Management Model Will Change

This is such a fundamental (and so frequently overlooked) element of crafting a successful Management Transition that it bears repeating. From generation to generation in any family business, the management model will change. It will change purposefully and with forethought, or it will change by accident in a test of wills.

But it will change. From generation to generation, and in every family business, the management model will change!

There are three models that typify the progressive changes in the family business management model:

- The first-generation model is the all-powerful founder. One person has all the ownership and authority, and is accountable to none but himself or herself.
- Ivan Lansberg calls the second-generation model the "Sibling Partnership." In this model, siblings share power and authority in some form—even if one is the top executive.
- If the family is still active in management, third generations and beyond are what Lansberg calls "Cousins Confederations."

## The Powerful Founder—The Single Decision Maker

This is simple. One person. The embodiment of the business. All the final authority. Every important decision (and many, if not most, less important decisions) eventually gets made—or at least approved—by the powerful founder. Founders have no responsibility to any constituents other than themselves.

## Second-Generation Management—Shared Decision-Making

A sibling is now occupying the top executive job. Having vested final authority in that person, the business enters the second generation of family business management. In the process, the parent-child relationship is being replaced by peer relationships.

The most significant change in the second-generation management model is the reality of shared power. Regardless of who is given the leadership "title," he or she now has a constituency of siblings who may have both ownership and management responsibilities. Clearly, they will expect to have a voice. They may even be able to "gang up" and oust the anointed leader if they become too dissatisfied.

Second-generation leaders face another reality. They may well find themselves either actually sharing some power with the founder, or having to live up to the memory of the founder.

On the positive side, all the siblings have grown up in the same family. They have been raised by the same parents, influenced by the same value system.

On the not-so-positive side, sibling rivalry can raise its ugly head. If siblings have been raised in a highly competitive family system, the struggle doesn't disappear or even fade in adulthood. In fact, it is often played out in the business to a degree that jeopardizes business prosperity. Here is an example of how that occurred in a very successful business:

Ted was a powerful founder running the business. Daughter Charlene and sons Adam and Brian all held management positions. They were competent, committed and cooperative, and the business was thriving. Suddenly Ted had a serious heart attack and left his daughter and sons to run the business.

A major power struggle broke out between the siblings. Dad came back to work against his doctor's advice and took control. Things calmed down; however, the tension between the siblings continued to affect their ability to work together.

In working with this family business, we were able to help them come to a critical realization. There were two reasons that the model Ted had created (one person with all the authority, responsible to no other constituents) wouldn't work:

1. The siblings had each other as constituents and were, therefore, responsible to each other.

2. They had never learned to operate as cooperative decision makers.

Once they fully understood the concept of shared power, a new management model was developed. This time the model included well- differentiated areas of responsibility and authority

Unfortunately, the model was tested two years later when Ted again became seriously ill. But the model worked! Ted was able to complete a full recovery, and is now back on a very limited basis in a greatly reduced role. Meanwhile, the business thrived in his absence and continues to thrive.

If you or your children are involved in a "sibling partnership," take heed and think this through together. In the abstract it may not be possible to describe your ideal management model. However, we do know that it will take a different form than that of the "powerful founder" model that characterized the first generation.

## Third Generation—And Beyond

Two new and different challenges await family businesses that transition into the third "Cousins Confederation" generation and beyond.

Cousins will have grown up in different family units with different parents and different value systems. In many extended families they will have had limited contact with other cousins, certainly less than with their siblings. So when cousins work together in a family business, they meet with less in common in their backgrounds.

The second major challenge is sheer size. Its a numbers game. One way of looking at it is that the number of siblings grows arithmetically, while the number of cousins grows exponentially. Most businesses will not be able to grow sufficiently to accommodate all the siblings in one owning family, let alone all the cousins in the extended family of owners. The choices about involvement, roles, responsibilities, representation, authority and power get more complex in each succeeding generation.

As a result of these realities, building the management model in the third generation and beyond involves five important processes:

1. Building trusting personal relationships among cousins
2. Reconciling different backgrounds, values and expectations
3. Reaching consensus about criteria for active involvement in the business
4. Providing adequate representation for a growing number of owners who are not directly involved in managing their family's business

5. Providing liquidity for those who believe that holding minority shares in a family business may not be their best investment vehicle

The fact that one approach may have worked well in the second-to third-generation transition is no guarantee that the same decisions and actions will effectively serve the next transition. However, with thoughtful planning the business can be maintained in the family for generations. And this is possible despite a growing number of family members. It is easy to find examples in the many family businesses now in the third and fourth generations of ownership.

Some of the more successful strategies they have employed include:

- Limiting the number of family members in active management by managing expectations, establishing firm guidelines for employment and defining career path options
- Increasing the reliance on nonfamily executives
- Placing greater emphasis on family participation in governance as opposed to management
- Using family wealth to fund new venture opportunities outside the family business for competent family members
- Creating other avenues for responsible family involvement (family foundations, for example)

If the family loses its family/business balance, the sheer numbers of people involved in any one of these later-generation transitions can make the situation unwieldy. There are many possible responses. Some families sell the business privately to outsiders, or to their employees through an ESOP. Others take their company public. Very often, one branch of the family buys out the other branches and the cycle starts over again.

In any event, this element of the Management Transition needs to be explicitly addressed in each generation. Many options are available. Whatever option you select can work with agreement, support and planning.

## Element #2: Options and Opportunities

The next step on the path to a successful and satisfying Management Transition involves making two key decisions:

**Key Decision 1:** What attributes constitute the ideal candidate?

**Key Decision 2:** How large will be the universe in which we intend to search for this candidate?

## The Ideal Candidate

There is no boilerplate set of specific attributes; no "universal" set of candidate specifications; no "one size fits all" description. Therefore, it is not possible to provide a specific, detailed prescription for an ideal candidate for your next top executive. What follows are three principles that will help you develop the specifications that work for you.

1. Start by re-reading your strategic business plan. Make sure you can define where the business is going over the longer term, and can identify the major challenges to be faced in getting there.
2. Determine what kind of person it will take to meet those challenges.
   - What knowledge base will the next top executive need to have to lead the charge?
   - What kinds of experience should the ideal executive have in his or her background?
   - What should be his or her primary skills, strengths and interests?
3. Now look at the "personality" of the business. What personal attributes should the next leader possess?

These are the essential questions. Answering them will not be as simple as you may think.

> *If you don't have a clearly articulated strategic vision and plan for your business, you will not be able to make a rational and responsible decision about candidate specifications!*

Now you can understand why we put the Business Transition before the Management Transition in our Six Transition succession-planning models.

## The Search Universe

There is a mystical tablet buried in the Mojave Desert, its location known only to family business founders age 60 and above. On it is inscribed the guiding principle of successor selection for many of those founders.

We have never actually seen it. However, based on the reality of many family businesses we have evaluated, it must look approximately like this:

> *My firstborn male child*
> *is the natural successor*
> *to the leadership position*
> *in the next generation*
> *of my family business.*

Word has it that this tablet is deteriorating at an increasingly rapid rate. We even know a couple of bold mystics who believe that it will be in barely recognizable pieces in just one more generation. This opinion, by the way, is met with loud cheers and applause from just about everyone in family businesses—except for firstborn sons, of course.

The mysterious tablet is a lighthearted way of introducing a serious issue. Deciding about how broadly—or how narrowly—you will draw the candidate search boundaries is a serious matter.

You have some obvious choices.

1. One is to opt for choosing your firstborn son.
   Primogeniture, the passage of assets to the firstborn male, has strong historical and traditional roots. We have met members of 12- and 13-generation family businesses who are firmly convinced that their survival would not have been possible without this rigid succession model. However, these are different times. We currently see many successful exceptions to this tradition, particularly with the increased participation of women in business. However, if the founder is undecided about choosing between children, reverting to established tradition feels like the easy way out. It could be an excellent choice, providing your firstborn son is a qualified candidate (or possesses the potential to become qualified).
2. A second option is to restrict the search to family members. This is another popular approach. It certainly keeps your business a "family business" in the truest sense of the term. It can be a good universe for your search if that universe is populated by qualified or potentially qualified candidates who want the job. We've heard and seen the downside.

This true story of a second son is our most vivid memory. He reported that *"Dad called me into his office to tell me I was his selection to be the next president. I told him I wasn't the right person for the job. Dad replied, 'Nonsense, you can do it,' and here I am, years later—floundering at doing something I don't want to be doing."*

3.  A third possibility is to seek the strongest possible candidate, family member or not. The strength of this approach is that it increases your options. Indeed, there may well be nonfamily candidates who are stronger leaders and better managers. If so, this would seem to be the appropriate choice in order to assure business prosperity. It may also be the choice that maintains harmony when several family members are campaigning for the top job. Certainly, we have seen many family businesses succeed under leadership from outside the bloodline. More than one family has wisely chosen an in-law as its business leader. Others have employed a nonfamily CEO accountable to a Board of Directors.

4.  In some families a decision has been made to specifically exclude family members from consideration, no matter their qualifications or interest. We mention this because it is a reality. It happens. However, this decision is typically a reaction to having heard horror stories of what can happen to families in business. The perspective and principles in *Hats Off to You — 2* can keep your family business from becoming one of the fatalities.

5.  We are now seeing increasing use of an alternative that provides another good illustration of "and/both" thinking in the search for balance. Many families arrive at the point of decision on a management successor, only to find that they have not done enough to prepare family candidates who have potential. For these families the issue is not "if" the successor can be qualified. Instead, the issue is "when" the successor will be ready. Rather than promote a potentially capable but inexperienced family member into the top executive role, they hire a nonfamily member to serve as an interim CEO. These interim executives typically have a timetable within which—in addition to running the business—they are expected to help groom a selected family member to take over.

## Element #3: Management Development

It is said that we all live in a fishbowl. That is certainly true of family members in management positions in a family business. In fact, the glass in their fishbowl is clearer than most. The words spoken by family members, the actions they take and the ways in which they behave (and misbehave) are watched closely by the entire employee population.

### The Enemy Is Us

We lead and manage by example. Therefore, the examples we provide set the tone for the entire business. More than once in our careers we have heard an executive complain, *"I am not pleased mth the way my subordinates are behaving. What is going on, what is causing it and what should I do about it?"*

The answer to this question lies in an understanding of what is really happening. Subordinates are behaving in ways they believe top management wants them to behave. We all have a strong survival instinct. In businesses, employees look "up" in the organization to see how their bosses behave. What are their work habits? What standards do they set for themselves? How do they treat other people (employees, customers and vendors)? The assumption is that survival depends upon the bosses' approval. The bosses set the standard, so they must be behaving the way they want their employees to behave. Using that rationale, your employees will adjust their behavior to emulate yours.

Finding the cause is fairly easy. Just get the managers together and look in a mirror. The "enemy" is us!

What can be done? Set standards that describe ideal behavior in your business. Then compare your behavior and that of your managers to this standard. Finally, help, encourage and require yourself and other managers to improve in those areas that don't meet the standard. That way, the next time employees look "up" the organization, they will see positive examples that will lead them to change their behavior. This is why it is so important to analyze the quality of the management development in family businesses.

### Management Is a Learned Skill

Based on what we have seen over the years, there seem to be a few very popular misconceptions at work in family businesses.

**Misconception 1: Family members learn effective management merely by osmosis.** A young adult comes to work in the family business. He or she starts from the ground up and is even rotated through all the departments. Along the way, however, this "manager in waiting" is given little guidance. He or she is not told what to look for in those experiences, i.e., what important lessons to learn in each step of that rotation. Therefore, our subject makes his or her own decisions about what is appropriate and important. Those decisions may be on target—or not. It becomes a game of chance.

**Misconception 2: Dad's or Mom's way of managing must be replicated.** This can be a very dangerous assumption. A word to the current leader: You have run a successful business for many years. Certainly you have made some mistakes, but you have run it your way, and that way worked for you. However, your successor will be dealing with the business at a different point and time in the business cycle. What was successful in the past may need to be changed somewhat to be effective in tomorrows business climate. Additionally, each individual practices the art and science of managing with his or her own unique strengths, styles and preferences.

This was clearly illustrated during one of the three-day seminars we conduct for family businesses. Among the participants were a father (named Sid for the purposes of this recounting) and his son and daughter, whom we'll call Matt and Carrie, Sid was the chief executive, Matt ran manufacturing and Carrie headed their retail division.

It was early in the weekend and we were all getting acquainted. Sid told the group that he and his wife had purchased a condo in Florida to which they intended to retire. Sid was ready to move. The only thing holding him back was some assurance that Matt and Carrie would be able to make "good" management decisions in his absence. Matt pointed out that both divisions were flourishing. Sid grudgingly confirmed that but said he was uncomfortable with the way his son and daughter made decisions. He felt that he had to continually second-guess them. Asked to elaborate, Sid let it be known that the assurance he was seeking was that Matt and Carrie would approach their decision making just as he did. He also wanted to be sure that they would make the same decisions he would make. Whereupon we advised Sid that he sell the condo because, under those terms, he would never get to live there.

**Misconception 3: Good managers are born that way.**
Although the saying is popular, it probably has never been true. It certainly cannot be true in today's business environment, in which managers must contend with:

- Rapid change
- Higher costs
- More discerning, demanding customers
- Growing opportunities to employ technology in the management process
- The challenge of selecting from more available information than any one person can possibly digest

Most young adults coming into the family business have a good formal education, and that is a good start. The challenge is learning to effectively apply that knowledge in a specific business. You can read all the books your can find about bicycle riding, but until you actually get on the bicycle . . .

### What to Do Next

This brings us to the importance of becoming serious about management training and development in your family business. It is in your enlightened self-interest to take the chance out of the game.

We have been involved with hundreds of family businesses. Too few of them had a formal, functioning management training and development program when we first began to work with them.

In the "what to do next" spirit of *Hats Off to You — 2*, here are some ideas to guide the design of an effective program.

- **Customize the program to meet unique individual needs.** To do this, you will need to make some decisions about likely career paths. The depth of understanding of the production process required of the next production executive is far greater than that required of an individual passing through production on his or her way to marketing or finance.
- **Don't stop at technical/functional competence.** These skills are important, but there is far more to management development than technical competence.
- **Include your value system and management process in the curriculum.** To perpetuate the values that drive your business, and the system by which they are applied, both must be defined and communicated. Generic management principles can be taught in the classroom. How they get applied in the business needs to be learned in the business in the context of its own unique management values and processes.
- **Build the management team.** As much as we advocate customizing a program for individual managers, these managers

do not work in a vacuum. Include elements that enhance communication and understanding among all members of management. Maintain a balance between individual initiative and group process. Both have a place in every enterprise.

- **Define the learning objectives of each development step.** You will be investing time and money in a purposeful development program. You deserve a good return on that investment. Help ensure it by making explicit just what perspective and knowledge an individual should be seeking.

**Follow-up Step A: Making the Decision**

> **A Great Truth:**
> *In order to have a successful Management Transition, there must be a management successor.*

The fact that the decision must be made will come as no great surprise. The more important matter is how the decision will be made. Here are some possibilities.

- **You and the possible candidates can work it out together.**
  These can be difficult discussions because everyone will have a direct stake in the outcome. However, if you are working hard on the Family Transition, you will have used family/business retreats to refine your problem-solving and consensus-building skills to the level needed for this approach to work. The advantage is that all those with direct interest in the decision will have participated in making it. Under those circumstances you are more likely to get the kind of buy-in that will assure the person selected will enjoy peer support.
- **Have the board of directors choose the successor.**
  This option is available if you have an active board that includes independent outside directors. This option works well in situations where there is more than one qualified candidate or where nonfamily and family candidates are both under consideration. The board adds a layer of objectivity to the selection process.
- **Involve the next generation in the selection process.**
  The supporting rationale for this approach is that they are the ones who will have to live with their choice.

### Follow-up Step B: Document the Plan

If the Management Transition were simply a matter of selecting a successor, you could make the decision and move on. But, as you can tell from reading this chapter, a successful Management Transition is a more comprehensive proposition. To do it well you must:

- Identify and make explicit those values by which you manage the enterprise
- Identify required leadership capabilities
- Define management processes and standards
- Develop and test a new management model for the next generation
- Design and implement a formal management development and training program

It is our strong recommendation that you commit the various elements of the Management Transition plan to writing as they are developed.

## Introduction to Chapters 5 and 6

In preparing the second edition of *Hats Off to You*, we thought it prudent to determine whether the changes in Federal estate tax laws enacted since the writing of the first edition invalidated any information contained in Chapter 5 (The Ownership Transition) and/or Chapter 6 (The Estate Transition). We asked tax and estate planning experts to review what we had written and advise us if any changes were required.

The consensus response was that no changes were required. The information contained in these chapters is concerned with fundamental principles rather than with planning techniques. These principles are provided to help guide business owners and their families; to help them understand the factors that should be considered in setting and agreeing upon goals for these two transitions. While tax laws have changed—and may continue to change—the principles remain as sound today as they were when the first edition was written. However, our discussions with tax and estate planning experts yielded two important considerations that warrant mention.

## Changes in Taxation Do Not Eliminate the Need to Plan

Many family business owners have viewed the change in estate tax tables as eliminating the need to plan for (and fund) the transfer of business ownership and their entire estate. While the prospects for savings in planning fees and life insurance premiums are tempting, reputable professionals whom we trust counsel that such savings are illusory. They advise that planning for ownership and estate transitions is as important now as it has ever been. There are two basic reasons supporting their position:

1.  The estate tax is a "hot item" on the political agenda and, when it comes to politics, the winds of change never stop blowing. There is no guarantee that the current estate tax laws will survive to the "magic year" of 2010. Even if they do, as it stands now, after 2010 estate tax liabilities will revert to what existed prior to current legislation having been enacted.

2.  Talk continues about the possibility of repealing the estate tax altogether. If that happens, the loss in income to the Federal government will be made up somehow. One very likely prospect is eliminating the step-up in cost basis that accrues to the next generation of business owners at the death of the senior generation. That will have a major impact on the future of family businesses. As one colleague

in Great Britain explained, "If that happens, you may have a system similar to ours. Our tax system makes it relatively easy and inexpensive to keep the business in the family, but decidedly expensive to take any cash out." In any event, even with today's estate tax schedules, and even in the face of uncertainty about the future of the estate tax itself, sound planning and funding of ownership and estate transfers is as important today as it has ever been.

### Take Time to Understand Your Plan

All too often, owners of family businesses pay good and trusted advisors to plan ownership and estate transfers and to document those plans. The plans are explained, the documents are filed and life goes on. At the beginning of every engagement, we ask our clients to summarize their ownership transfer and estate plans. The most frequent answer given goes something like this: "I have a plan, but I don't remember how it works." And when a family business owner can't remember his or her own ownership and estate transition plans, chances are the rest of the family doesn't know.

One of our partners Ed Cox's favorite maxims about family businesses is that "mystification leads to alienation." When ownership and estate transition plans are not understood by the founder or current leader and/ or are not communicated to the rest of the family, then mystification exists in at least this part of the family business system. That leaves a knowledge gap, and that gap opens the door for conflict in the family business system.

We are mindful of the disruptive role conflict plays in attempts to maintain effective relationships in family businesses. We have this advice for owners and their advisors:

**For Owners:** Make sure you really understand the ownership and estate transition plans developed by your advisors. Verbal explanations are commonplace occurrences when plans are completed, but they are not the entire answer. What you heard in the attorney's office, for example, may make sense at the time but is hard to recall months later. Ask your advisors for, and make sure you receive, a written summary in "plain English."

**For Advisors:** Do your clients a favor. If they don't ask for a written summary of your work in language that is easy to understand, insist that they not leave your office without one.

*""The horror of that moment,'*
*the King went on,*
*I shall never, never forget!'*
*'You will, though,' the Queen said,*
*'if you don't make a memorandum of it.'"*

LEWIS CARROLL
*Through the Looking-Glass*
1872

## CHAPTER FIVE

# *The Ownership Transition*

Once you have made the decisions required to complete the Management Transition, you know who will run the business in the next generation. Now you are in a good position to answer the principal question of the Ownership Transition:

> **Who will control the business
> in the next generation?**

The four most critical elements in planning the Ownership Transition are:

#1. Challenge assumptions
#2. Understand the differences between "fair" and "equal"
#3. Document your decisions #4. Strengthen the ownership team

## Element #1: Challenge Assumptions

The "going in" assumption for the vast majority of our family business clients is that the family will continue to both own and manage the business in the next generation. In principle, we applaud that assumption because of our belief in the importance of family-owned businesses. We are professionally committed to assisting in the successful perpetuation of family-owned businesses. At the same time, we encourage the idea of testing assumptions to make sure they are feasible.

In chapter 3 we introduced the idea of strategic planning for the business. One of the keys to success in that effort is a willingness to challenge every assumption upon which you currently do business. Assumptions which stand up to challenge are building blocks for the future. Those which do not withstand challenge need to be replaced.

We view a balanced succession planning process as strategic planning for the family. Thus, it is only prudent to challenge whatever assumptions your family has made about ownership in the next generation. If they withstand the challenge, then go for it. If they don't, then consider changing the course of the future.

Our experience leads us to believe that blindly following an assumption that continued ownership is the only thing to do has contributed to many failed family businesses.

Any one of the following signals may indicate other ownership options should be considered:

- As a result of your Management Transition decisions, you have determined that nonfamily leadership is the best choice for the long term.
- The business needs to retain profits to sustain itself, but the owners and/or future owners have high income demands.
- Some owners want to sell their shares, and there is no obvious way for either the business or the other owners to fund the purchases.
- There is no one in the next generation who is interested in or knowledgeable about the business.

**Consider All Reasonable Alternatives**

The obvious alternatives to sustaining exclusive family ownership of the business are either a private sale to outside buyers or a public offering. If all the owners want liquidity, these may be the only options you need to consider.

In many family businesses, however, it is not that easy. More often, when the "let's keep it all in the family" assumption is challenged, it is because some, but not all, owners want to sell and some, but not all, owners want to retain their ownership positions.

There are other options. They may not all be acceptable or feasible in your family business, but they do exist and should be considered. They permit full or partial sales, while maintaining some continued family involvement—or even control. Here are just a few examples of strategies available to family businesses.

- Keep the business in the family, but use nonfamily managers and use shared ownership or profits as incentives.
- Restructuring the entity as an "S" corporation would allow flow-through of profits to inactive owners.
- Sell to those senior managers who have demonstrated the capacity to operate the business successfully. They may not have the financial capacity to "cash out" the owners. However, if they are competent, consider a sale over time funded by future profits. This approach can reward the loyalty and talent that helped build the business. On the downside, it subjects the sellers to continued economic risk that they might prefer to avoid. Despite that, it may still be an attractive alternative, particularly if this is the best way to assure the future value of the business.
- Sell to the entire employee group through an Employee Stock Option Plan (an "ESOP"). Under the right circumstance, ESOPs provide sellers with attractive tax benefits. But there are negative features as well, not the least of which is the effort and costs of administering the plan. Look carefully before leaping into an ESOP.
- Sell a major stake to outside venture capitalists. Remember, however, that their primary objective is to build value and resell the business as quickly as possible. Make sure their exit strategy supports your exit strategy.
- Sell a major stake in the business to a strategic partner. Unlike most venture capitalists, strategic partners will have longer-term investment horizons. They will be motivated by opportunities to reduce competition, assure market resources, capture technology, and so on.
- Sell to one or more of the founder's (or current owner's) children who have demonstrated the desire and competency to continue the business. One outcome of this option is to reduce tension between active and inactive owners in the next generation. When the owner completes his or her estate transition, some of the cash from the sale can be given to the children who don't own the business. This can help equalize the value received from the estate. But there may be arguments about how the business is valued for sale, tax implications, perceived favoritism, etc.

There are no easy choices. When considering any option, be sure to get advice from knowledgeable experts.

## Element #2: "Fair" May Not Be "Equal" (And "Equal" May Not Be "Fair")

The Vancouver Chapter of the Canadian Association for Family Enterprise (CAFE) produced an excellent video entitled Fairness vs. Equal. It is well worth watching if you are working on the Ownership Transition. It takes place in the aftermath of the death of a business founder. In brief, it tells the story of the very unfortunate consequences of an equal division of business ownership among the deceased founder's four children—only one of whom was active in managing the family business.

Although the sibling running the business was competent and committed, the personal demands of his new "equal" partners ultimately forced a sale of the business.

Our position is that the issue of who should own stock in the next generation is one of those questions for which the fulcrum should be moved toward the business end of the balance beam. But how far?

### What About Control?

Conventional wisdom often suggests that voting control of the stock in a family business should rest with those individuals who are active in the business. The most popular supporting example assumes the founder divides the stock among his or her heirs. That typically creates two groups of related owners: (1) those who are active in management and are receiving compensation, benefits and—very often—substantial perquisites for their efforts; and (2) inactive owners who can look only to dividends or distributions for current income.

Given the above hypothetical ownership situation, assume that management makes a sound, defensible business decision to forego dividends or cash distributions in order to reinvest in the business. The inactive shareholders become angry with their relatives for making a completely appropriate business decision.

When inactive shareholders are unhappy with active family management, they find ways to vent their frustrations and make everyone's life miserable in the process. Here are some retaliatory tactics we have seen unhappy owners employ:

- A "hate mail" campaign: *"I'll write a slew of angry letters to my siblings in management and copy everyone."*
- The letter from the lawyer: *"I'll have my attorney draw up one of those nasty letters full of veiled threats and dump it*

*on his or her desk. That will keep the \*%^!# off balance!"*

- Alienation: *"I won't go to their family celebrations, and won't invite them to ours. That will teach them a lesson!"*
- Loss of visitation: *"You can't see your nieces and nephews (or your grandchildren). Your kids can't play with my kids."*

## Forget Control, What About Ownership In General?

Another frequently mentioned concept is to distribute all the stock in the business only to active family members, and to give non business assets to the inactive family members. The rationale for this option is as follows: If you were deciding to invest cash equivalent in value to the stock you've been given, would you really buy stock that:

1. Paid very small dividends
2. Paid them only sporadically
3. Was not traded in any organized market
4. Could only be sold to certain people after certain events, e.g., death, disability or divorce
5. Was priced below market value
6. Could only be sold over time on so-so terms?

Any rational human being would answer no. To the extent that this description fits many family businesses, one could argue that giving inactive family members any stock at all is doing them a disservice.

What are the problems with this option? The first, and most obvious, is that many family business owners do not have sufficient nonbusiness assets to make "fair" decisions about ownership transfer and still equalize the distribution of their entire estate.

Another concern is that valuing the family business can be a bit tricky. Family members active in the business may maintain that the value of the business will drop after the founder's death. Or they will argue that the higher the value, the higher the estate taxes. Both of those arguments are intended to support keeping the value down. Those outside the business will be wary of any attempt to reduce the business's value—for fear that the active family members will be gaining an unfair advantage. Reaching agreement under those circumstances is difficult at best.

An additional issue is that some inactive family members may really want to own a piece of the family business for one of more of the following reasons. The business:

- Is performing well
- Has a bright future

- Is well managed
- Is paying meaningful dividends
- Could provide employment opportunities for heirs
- Has the potential to be sold for a significant gain

A family business such as this is both a good current investment and a potentially valuable long-term asset. Loss of ownership would mean leaving both the income and appreciation to others.

Finally, some family members who are currently active in the business may actually prefer a piece of the nonbusiness assets. For example, the idea of owning income-producing real estate that is handled by a management company can be very appealing to a family business executive who has just put in a 14-hour day—for the 10th day in a row. Or perhaps the family business is not positioned for longer-term success. If that is the case, stock in the business could be a burden and the non-business assets a blessing.

### Aren't Taxes a Consideration?

Absolutely! Any decision with meaningful dollars involved must take prevailing tax laws into consideration. In general, anyone would want to do that which is most tax efficient. To do otherwise just doesn't make good sense. Suppose, however, that you are faced with two choices:

1. The most tax-efficient answer to ownership transfer that disrupts the balance between business prosperity, family harmony and personal well-being; or
2. A slightly less tax-efficient answer that is the most balanced of the two options.

Tax efficiency is only part of the process of ownership transfer.

### Whose Decision Is It, Anyway?

"Fairness" in ownership transfer decisions, as in most things in life, is in the eye of the beholder. Having said that, our position is that everyone who has a stake in the decision should have a voice.

Your professional advisors know the tax code and the most tax-efficient means for transferring ownership. But neither they nor you are as fully informed about how the potential recipients feel as are the recipients themselves. Explore options together. This is an excellent discussion topic for a family retreat.

## Element #3: Put It in Writing

Your ownership transfer decisions will ultimately find their way into your estate plan. But that is part of the sixth and final transition. Right now were still on transition number five—the Ownership Transition.

We have had the privilege of working on many family business engagements with Douglas K. Freeman, an attorney in the greater Los Angeles area. Doug believes that family businesses really need to write three Ownership Transition plans: the "sailing into the sunset plan," the "wheelchair plan" and the "drop dead plan."

The **Sailing into the Sunset Plan** is the one that owners prefer. It assumes the owner's voluntary gradual withdrawal or planned retirement. The plan covers those issues that will be important as the owner becomes increasingly less active in the business:

- Who will manage the business, and how will the selection be made?
- How will he, she or they be compensated?
- What are the retiring owner's financial needs and how will they be met?

The **Wheelchair Plan** is considerably less popular. It is the plan that should be in place to cover a sudden and unexpected disability. The same questions raised in the "Sunset Plan" should be answered in the "Wheelchair Plan." But because there is no way to know if or when the owner will become disabled, it is necessary to plan in anticipation of such an event. The feelings of shock and loss that occur as a result of an owner becoming disabled can be similar to the feelings experienced at a death. In many respects they are more difficult because the owner is still here, albeit unable to function as he or she once did. In any event, the smart move is to decide explicitly what would happen in your family business if such a circumstance arises. Generalized thoughts, hopes and wishes won't suffice.

The **Drop Dead Plan** is easily the least popular of the three—but necessary nonetheless. The event of death is inevitable (despite the readiness of many business founders and leaders to deny this reality). An unexpected death (an airplane accident, for example) is one challenge. The acid test for any business is whether everyone in management knows what they will do if the call comes in that the founder has died suddenly and unexpectedly. A death that can be anticipated (from disease or old age, for instance) poses similar but less time-critical challenges.

### Ownership Transfer Before Death

A founder's death does not have to trigger an ownership change if that transfer has been completed before death. Completing the first four transitions (Founder, Family, Business and Management) can facilitate a transfer of business ownership before the founder's or current leader's death. Some of the greatest successes in family businesses are testimonials to the benefit of timely succession planning.

## Ownership Transfer After Death

If the transfer of business ownership takes place at or after the current owners death, there are a variety of strategies that may be used. Each one has its own advantages and disadvantages. The two most prominent approaches are the following:

- A buy-sell agreement can assure the ownership transition by creating: (1) a ready and obligated buyer; (2) a known price or method of determining price; (3) payment terms; and (4) pre-arranged procedures. The issues related to the sale may be difficult to resolve during the planning stage. But, once resolved and documented, the implementation of the sale is greatly facilitated. We will explore the more important issues related to buy-sell agreements in the section on "Buy-Sell Basics" below.

- The business can be retained in the estate or trust of the decedent. While so held, it can provide for the heirs and be managed according to a prescribed structure. This gives the representatives of the decedent (executors or trustees) time to arrange for a smooth transition. Transition options include continued family management and ownership, nonfamily management under family governance, strategic partnerships or sale to outside third parties. The key to this strategy is timely selection of the individual (or individuals) who will have fiduciary responsibility for making prudent ownership decisions and assuring the heirs of fair treatment. These may or may not be the same fiduciaries responsible for the administration of the rest of the decedents estate. Possible candidates include family or nonfamily executives in the business; family members familiar with the business; business colleagues; professional advisors or professional fiduciaries, e.g., banks or trust companies.

## Buy-Sell Basics

We'll cover just the basics. It won't be technical, because we're not business lawyers and that isn't the purpose of this book. For more specific details contact your legal and/or financial advisors.

There are two types of buy-sell agreements. One is a cross-purchase agreement in which shareholders buy stock from each other at certain triggering events. The other is a corporate purchase agreement in which the business is the buyer or buyer of last resort.

Either type of agreement can be funded. Funding sources include a sinking fund, an ESOP or life insurance. Unfunded plans can provide extended payment terms that enable stockholders and/or the business to self-fund the repurchase obligation over time.

Cross-purchase or corporate purchase and funded or unfunded are but two of the major decisions required when developing a buy-sell agreement. Other significant decisions include:

1. What event(s) trigger action under the agreement (death? disability? withdrawal? retirement?)
2. How the value of the stock will be established (by periodic appraisal? by a set formula?)
3. Who can/must purchase stock
4. Whether stock can be sold to outsiders and, if so, under what terms and conditions
5. How to secure payment
6. Actions to be taken if a buyer defaults
7. How much stock each party can/must purchase
8. Who will track ownership and control the process
9. Terms of purchase

Perhaps the most significant decision faced by the owners is whether the agreement should allow the estate of a deceased shareholder to retain the stock, or to require redemption by the business and/or surviving owners. In other words, is the buy-sell mandatory or optional? And, if it is optional, who has the option—the prospective buyer or the estate?

On the next page you will find a succinct summary in tabular form. The form and content were provided by David Goldstein, a good and trusted friend in the insurance and financial services profession. We are sharing it with you with his permission—for which we are grateful.

## From the standpoint of the estate of the deceased shareholder:

| Retain | Redeem |
|---|---|
| **Advantages:** | **Advantages:** |
| • Possible appreciation of value for the family | • Known value or method to determine value and terms |
| • Source of income for family | • Liquidity for survivors |
| • Entry of heirs into business | • Diversification of risk |
| | • Avoid family conflict/rivalry |
| **Disadvantages:** | **Disadvantages:** |
| • Diluted control | • No future growth |
| • Indefinite income | • Disassociation with business |
| • Limited marketability | • Loss of ownership tradition |

## From the standpoint of the business and surviving shareholders:

| Retain | Redeem |
|---|---|
| **Advantages:** | **Advantages:** |
| • No commitment to buy | • Own all future growth |
| • No commitment to pay | • Less diverse owner expectations |
| • Avoid fight over value | |
| | **Disadvantages:** |
| **Disadvantages:** | • Must establish value |
| • Diverse owner expectations | • Need cash for purchases (either personal assets, business profits or cash flow) |
| • Growth shared with inactive owners | |
| • Possible dissident minority shareholders | |

## Element #4: Strengthen the Ownership Team

In chapter 3 on the Family Transition, we introduced the Owner hat as but one of the 15 principal hats any family member might have in his or her hat collection. Strength among the ownership team is developed by ensuring that everyone who has an owner hat knows how to wear it correctly.

### Ownership Rights

The specific rights of owners should be spelled out in the bylaws of the business. Most often, ownership rights are limited to:

- Electing directors
- Voting on specified major decisions (acquisitions, sale of the business, etc.)
- Expecting a fair return in return for the risks assumed.

Even with those basic rights, we are constantly confronted with shareholders who:

- Have never read the bylaws of the business they own
- Have never voted to elect directors
- Cannot provide their definition for a "fair return" on investment
- Will not (or cannot) share in the risks of ownership— which, in most family businesses, means personal guarantees

Note that this list of ownership rights does not include "meddling" in operations, making management decisions or an automatic seat on the board.

### Ownership Responsibilities

Owners have a responsibility to each other to make informed and reasoned decisions, and to know and respect limits of authority. To do so, each owner must have access to the information required to make informed decisions. They must also possess the competency to use that information once it gets into their hands.

### Shareholder Development

Competency levels may vary considerably among owners. We repeatedly see three unfortunate realities.

1. Far too many family business owners can't read or interpret a financial statement. If they are unwilling to learn, they must: depend on others to tell them what all the numbers mean. They become frustrated by changes they don't fully understand, and suspicious of the interpreters.

2. Those who can read and interpret financial statements get frustrated with those who cannot. A typical reaction is to withhold information, on the theory that the "incompetent" owners could not use it even if they had it.
3. Nobody does anything to change the equation.

Mistrust and frustration grow. Responsible ownership decisions are replaced with emotional decisions. As a result, the quality and strength of the ownership team is ultimately diminished.

The need for a plan and program to develop ownership competency is one of the most overlooked elements of the ownership transition. The stakes can be high. The rationale is expressed by this simple equation:

> *Competent Owners*
> *plus*
> *Informed Owners*
> *equals*
> *Responsible Ownership*

*"'Begin at the beginning,'*
*said the King gravely.*
*'And go 'til you come to the end;*
*then stop.'"*

LEWIS CARROLL
*Alice's Adventures in Wonderland*
1865

## CHAPTER SIX

# *The Estate Transition*

We have arrived at the last stop in our journey through the six succession transitions. As a reward for having come this far, we are going to spare you a recitation of estate tax tables, rules and regulations. We won't cite a single section of the tax code. You can get all that information from your estate planners and tax advisors. They know the rules and how to apply them.

Our goal in this brief chapter is to expand your perspective. Once you have a broad perspective about the Estate Transition, you will be able to use the services of your estate planners and tax advisors more effectively. With the proper perspective you can be a responsible architect of the Estate Transition. You will be able to more effectively articulate the outcomes you desire. Then you will want your professional advisors to put the right implementation vehicles in place. You want them to be the builders, to use their technical knowledge and skills to deliver an estate plan that rounds out and supports the balance between business prosperity, family harmony and personal well-being.

### We're Glad You Asked

Two questions often asked about this part of our Six Transitions model are:

1. Are not the Ownership and Estate Transitions one and the same? and

2. Why do you separate them in the Six Transition's model?

The answer to the first question is *"No, they are not."*

The answer to the second question is *"We separate them because they are different; close, but different."* It is an accurate answer that deserves further elaboration.

A more complete response is that the Ownership Transition concerns only the business assets in your estate. Remember our family/business balance bar? Ownership Transition decisions that promote balance are best made by moving the fulcrum closer to the "business" end of that bar.

The Estate Transition, on the other hand, includes consideration of your entire estate. Keep in mind that, in its entirety, your estate consists of both business and nonbusiness assets. Family interests are the heavier of the two weights for this transition. For example, the concept of equitability prevailed in our discussion of the Ownership Transition. In contrast, in the vast majority of families, Estate Transition decisions will be driven by the quest for equality.

The four essential elements of a balanced Estate Transition are:

#1. Orderly transitions

#2. Continuity

#3. Liquidity

#4. Legacy

Develop a clear vision of what you want with respect to these four factors. Communicate that vision to who ever is designing your estate plan. When those professionals understand your vision, they will be more efficient about producing a more effective product.

## Element #1: Orderly Transitions

The decisions you made during the Business and Management Transitions provide for business continuity. Handling those transitions effectively protects the assets that produce wealth for the family. The Ownership Transition decisions determined how business assets would be owned and controlled. Now, in the Estate Transition, you are seeking to divide your entire estate. If you are searching for equality, the path is easier if you first know who will own what portions of the business assets, and what they are worth.

By way of example, the representative of a family business recently called to seek our help. Her description of the reason the family had asked her to contact us was as follows: *"We have been working with Mom and Dad's lawyers on their estate plan. There are a number of questions for which we haven't been able to agree upon an answer. We're stuck, and Mom and Dad aren't getting any younger."* We met and spent time taking her through the Six Transition model. After hearing us out, her response was: *"I see the problem. We started at the wrong end."*

We could have given her the advice the King gave Alice: *"Begin at the beginning . . ."*

## Element #2: Continuity

Estate planners do important work. However, we have seen too many examples of added challenges visited on family businesses as the result of myopic estate planning. When a tax-focused founder attaches himself or herself to a tax-focused estate planner, what usually goes by the boards is **balance** in the family business. Note the following two examples.

The first instance involves a founder with competent adult offspring managing a successful business. The founder proudly described his estate plan as follows: *"My advisor has established generation-skipping insurance trusts that will give my grandchildren the cash to buy all the stock in the family business from the surviving spouse. I have also provided for nonfamily trustees."*

In addition to some tax implications for the surviving spouse, this approach to estate planning was an emotional time bomb ready to explode. Sooner or later his offspring who were running the business were going to discover a glitch that impacted them. They were investing their lives managing a business they would never own. And they could be fired by their sons, daughters, nieces and nephews—who may grow up to have minimal interest in the business.

A second composite profile is typical of many founder's ownership and estate transfer plans:

- The founder has six children, three of whom are active in the business.
- The founder gifts nonvoting common stock to all six children in equal proportion during his lifetime, and retains voting stock. The value of all shares will increase proportionately as the company grows. The voting common ensures the founder's continued control during his or her lifetime.
- There are provisions in the buy-sell agreement for puts and calls. Exercise of either is at the discretion of each stockholder. However, if an inactive stockholder elects to exercise his or her put option, the company must buy it out of cash flow. If the active stockholders elect to exercise their call options, the inactive owners must sell. Terms in each case are 10% cash down and the balance over some number of years.

At this point this plan sounds very professional. As a matter of fact, the concept is a favorite of some of the best estate planners we know. However, we found that this composite example failed to address the following continuity and family harmony issues:

- There is no relationship between the number of shares that may be redeemed at any one time and the ability of the business to pay for those shares. The business is strong today, but will the cash flow and/or borrowing power be there tomorrow? If it isn't, business continuity may be the price that is ultimately paid.
- Some of the inactive owners question the management ability of one or more of the active owners, and they have a valid concern. But the founder put management in place and the inactive owners are powerless on this and other issues during the founder's lifetime. If the founder is open to confronting competency issues during his or her lifetime, there is hope. If you have to wait until after the founder's death, things may get ugly.
- Because the control of the business still rests with the founder, the other owners are owners in name only. They are not required to make ownership decisions, so they don't learn the obligations of responsible ownership through practice. Rarely do we come across a family business that has taken the time to teach owners what ownership is really all about. Cooperation among six owners is a challenge, particularly if they don't learn the art of productive confrontation, compromise and consensus building.
- What if nonactive shareholders see potential for the business and don't want to be forced to sell?
- Can these six individuals work as a team? Has anyone seen evidence of this? Don't assume a cooperative ownership team will magically develop after the founder's death.

As with any of the myriad estate-planning techniques available, this example has its place in the right situations. It is the choice of advisors that becomes critical. Estate-planning professionals who take a balanced view of the succession process will often design estate plans that are sensitive to all the concerns pertinent to their family business clients.

By way of review, successful completion of the Estate Transition depends on five considerations: Remember that Estate Transition decisions:

1. Are driven more by family considerations than by business considerations
2. Ensure business continuity
3. Build the family's communication and problem-solving skills
4. Strengthen the potential ownership team
5. Then, and only then, provide for equality

## Element #3: Liquidity

Liquidity is an important component of the succession process. The reality is:

- You can't escape the fact that ownership of your assets is eventually going to be transferred.
- It doesn't make any difference how tax-efficient and creative you and your advisors are; sooner or later some transfer costs will be incurred by someone.
- Start transferring appreciating assets sooner rather than later. (We have worked with too many clients who started ownership and estate transfers after the value of the assets in their estates had grown substantially. No matter how hard they try and how creative their advisors, they can't get enough value transferred in the time they have left to avoid crippling transfer taxes.)
- If there isn't enough cash to pay those transfer costs out of pocket, some assets will have to be sold.
- If the uncovered transfer costs are too high, one of the assets your survivors will have to sell may be the business you have worked so hard to build.

> **Don't let that happen unless you want it to!**

- One or more family business owners may want to sell their interest. Financial provisions for their exit will protect family harmony and business continuity.

You and your family may have decided to sell the business. That decision is one possible result of your family's open deliberations about the Business, Management and Ownership Transitions. If that is your plan, then keep the family in control of the process. Sell it on your terms. Don't get trapped into a forced sale to satisfy the IRS. Businesses sold because the owners have no alternative rarely command top dollar. Seek advice from well-qualified professionals.

## Element #4: Legacy

Some family business owners favor keeping the business in the family. Their "legacy" will be a successful business that the family can continue to own and manage, and from which they will derive both income and increasing value. That is an admirable legacy provided there are those in the family who are interested in the business, competent to lead and manage it, and prepared to be responsible owners.

Others talk in terms of selling the business so that their "legacy" will be liquid wealth that their survivors can enjoy and employ as they wish. This is also a notable legacy—except in the eyes of those who are passionate about the business and are thereby denied the chance to continue that passion.

Remember that an individual's personal vision of a "legacy" may not be viewed with enthusiasm by all of his or her heirs. Developing a legacy that is attractive to the whole family signals that the "Success" in family business succession has be achieved.

We define the ideal as being a vision about legacy that is a direct result of balance and is not dependent on a "keep" or "sell" decision:

> ***We did what was best***
> ***for both the business and the family.***
> ***As a result, we can***
> ***perpetuate the family business tradition,***
> ***walk away winners or both!***

## An Ideal Legacy for a Family Business

Balanced Ownership and Estate Transition decisions, supported by successful resolution of the four preceding transitions, can make this legacy a reality.

### You can really have it all!

- Family members who are competent leaders and managers, who are passionate about the business, who have evaluated the risks and rewards and who have options can choose to keep the family business tradition intact.

- Family members who are not interested in the business, who know the risks and rewards and who have options can choose to divest themselves of management responsibility and ownership.

- Both can coexist with balanced succession planning. Individual family members can choose either option without anger or hurt feelings when the family understands that one legacy is not necessarily "right" for everyone, and has made the necessary provisions for both options.

- Both choices can be implemented because the family has learned to communicate effectively with each other about important issues. Business prosperity, family harmony and personal well-being are thus preserved.

> *From our perspective, legacies just don't get any better than that!*

*"There is a strange charm
in the thoughts of a good legacy,
or the hopes of an estate
which wondrously alleviates
the sorrow that men would otherwise
feelfor the death of friends."*

MIGUEL DE CERVANTES
*Don Quixote de la Mancha*
1615

## CHAPTER SEVEN

# *Closing Thoughts*

You now have learned the essential elements of our Six Transitions and understand the order of the game plan. We hope that the investment of the time it took to read the first six chapters has given you:

- **Perspective** about a new, fresh, practical view of family business succession
- **Understanding** that succession is a lifelong process that is repeated in each generation
- **Appreciation** for the comprehensiveness of the succession challenges in your family business—in any family business
- **Insight** into the key elements of each transition; the "critical few" decisions that families must make in order to achieve balance and find the "success" in succession
- **Knowledge** that there are points in the process at which there will be a need to access professional advice
- **Recognition** that greater value will be received from the efforts of professional advisors if the "critical few" decisions associated with each transition have been made and are communicated to them

**What It Takes**

Our part of the bargain is to provide the information we believe you need to gain perspective, understanding, appreciation, insight, knowledge and recognition. You have the option of either acting on what you have gained—or not.

There are a few additional thoughts we want to share that will position you to implement an action plan. We like the advice given by Alan Boal in *The Able Navigator*. With his permission, we've adapted a portion of The Able Navigator that addresses the "five V's" of leadership. We've also added a sixth and seventh " V" These are attributes that will help families achieve balance.

- **Vision**

  Successful family business transitions depend upon a shared understanding of where you are going. Define what your dreams are as a family and for the business you own. Remember, unless you know your destination, you may end up in the wrong place.

- **Values**

  While vision is what leaders stand for, values are what leaders stand on. Your family needs a shared recognition of the principles that guide your lives and drive your business.

- **Vocation**

  Being involved in a family business is more than a job or a pay-check. If you really belong here, it is because of something far deeper than merely a quest for power, reward, status and title. To achieve continued success, the family business needs to become a way of life for which you must have a passion and are willing to make compromises. In other words, you must view it as a vocation of choice.

- **Vehicles**

  In The Able Navigator, this attribute is known as "vessels." It goes well with the title. Boal points out that Walt Disney's vision was to have a clean, wholesome place were he could take his daughters on weekends. The Magic Kingdom—a clean, whole some place where anybody could take their children—became the vehicle that enabled Disney to realize his vision. Your family business started as the vehicle by which the founder hoped to realize a vision. Perpetuating the business requires that the family regards the business as a vehicle through which it can realize its collective vision.

- **Viability**

  Hats Off to You is about both people and businesses. Think of your vision as your destination and your business as the vehicle transporting you. It is essential that your business be operationally and financially viable. The "vehicle" has to be in good working condition.

- **"Voice**

  There are two aspects to voice. One is personal voice. The other is the voice of leadership. At the personal level is the attribute of open, honest, constructive communication. It is a vital part of the success equation. Family members must be able to talk with one another. They must feel safe to talk openly and honestly about the real issues and to engage in constructive problem solving. If they can, then you will find answers to the key questions that drive each succession transition. Leadership is the articulate voice that motivates and moves the company and the family forward.

- **Volition**

  If "guts" began with a "v", it would have been our word of choice. As you've probably already experienced, getting into balance in a family business is hard work. Like a business, it has its moments—its ups and downs. There are no quick fixes. Everyone one in the family must understand this from the beginning. It takes a strong sense of volition to get through the rough spots.

## 12 Rules for Success

These 12 rules for family business success represent the collective experience of hundreds of successful family businesses we know personally.

| For the Founder/Leader |
| :---: |
| **Rule #1** |
| **Create a Vision...Share the Vision** |

In your role of founder or current leader, take the lead and involve the family in creating a three- to five-year vision for the business. In your role as executive, involve other managers in charting the course that will make the vision a reality.

| **Rule #2** |
| :---: |
| **Change . . . Willingly** |

As your business evolves, make sure the roles you play evolve with it. The management skills and style that helped get your business started may not be those that are needed to support a larger, more mature organization.

Plan ahead for your own transition and for management succession. Don't let it happen by default. Make sure your firm grip on the business doesn't become a stranglehold. Finally, remember that you can die in the saddle, but it is very hard on the horse!

---
**For the Family**

---
**Rule #4**

---
**Promote Good Family Relationships**

---

Healthy family relationships and open communication drive the family business forward. Conflict-centered family relationships and ineffective communication drive the family business backward. No family business is in neutral.

---
**Rule #5**

---
**Keep Your Values in Balance!**

---

Families and businesses use different values. Make sure your family values don't dictate the way the business is run; and don't allow business values to dictate the way the family runs. "Either/or" thinking creates unbalanced family businesses. "And/both" thinking creates balance. Work as a family to support the best business practices, and work as a business to provide the best rewards you can for the family. Create a family creed that documents the decisions you have made to keep the family and business in balance.

---
**Rule #6**

---
**Build the Family Business Team!**

---

Establish the rules by which you play the business "game." Determine what positions you need, the role of each position and who is going to play those positions. Then learn how to work smarter together as a team.

## For the Firm

### Rule #7

### Take Care of the Culture!

Leaders only lead with the consent of their followers. Be a leader who merits respect! A going business is "going" because of its people. Make your company a place where people want to work, excel and contribute. They will do more than what is expected of them if you will recognize more of what they do.

### Rule #8

### Optimize Your Resources

Take a balanced approach to managing the resources of both the business and the family. Know when and how much to invest in the business, and when and how much to invest in the family. Your family deserves a good lifestyle, but not at the expense of the business.

### Rule #9

### Position, Position, Position!

Keep your business positioned with the right products and right services in the right markets. If you can't be first in a category, then create a new category! Most people know Charles Lindbergh and what he achieved. Who remembers the second person to fly solo across the Atlantic? Differentiate your firm to sustain a competitive advantage. Know which products and markets to support, and which to avoid or let go. Manage change; don't let change manage you.

## For the Future

### Rule #10

### Provide for Tomorrow's Leadership Today

New business challenges require new management skills. One of the liabilities of family business is the failure to adapt the business to changing environments. A second failure is the lack of clearly defined leadership development. Family members often don't rise through the ranks. Instead they are arbitrarily assigned management roles for which they may not be prepared. Assure continuity of management today. Plan now to put the right people in the right places, and prepare them for the roles they must play.

---
### Rule #11
### Plan to Transfer Ownership!
---

Make certain that ownership of the family business is transferred by design, not by default. Keep control of the business in the hands of the family members who are directly involved in the business. Make sure you have made good ownership transfer decisions (see chapter 5) before completing your estate plan (see chapter 6). Make your ownership and estate transfer plans tax sensitive but legacy driven.

---
### Rule #12
### Keep Some Financial Eggs in Other Baskets
---

Make certain that your financial security in retirement is not entirely dependent on the continued success of the business. Use tax-effective approaches to provide retirement income. Develop a financial plan that will enable you to invest outside the business to diversify your personal portfolio. Financial freedom and independence is the vision most founders and families have today. The best strategy for achieving financial independence is to diversify now.

## A Concluding Thought

Achieving balance and keeping your dreams alive in a family business are both possible when you master the Six Transitions we have shared with you in this book.

We can lead ourselves and others if we keep in mind that everyone in the family business is a unique individual. We lead strongest when we create community, respect individuality and empower all family members to be the best they can. All these ideas can be summarized in the poetry of Kahlil Gibran. In *The Prophet*, Gibran wrote:

> *...But let there be spaces in your togetherness*
> *and let the winds of heaven dance between you.*
> *...Sing and dance together and be joyous,*
> *but let each one of you be alone,*
> *Even as the strings of a lute are alone*
> *though they quiver with the same music.*
> *.. .And stand together, yet not too near together:*
> *For the pillars of the temple stand apart,*
> *And the oak tree and cypress grow not in each other's shadow.*

PART III

*Practical Tools*

# OVERVIEW OF THE 8 PRACTICAL TOOLS

## Practical Tool 1
### *Profiling Your Family Business System*

Succession planning is really strategic planning for the family business system. As with strategic business planning, when working to find the right paths for your family business in the succession planning process, it helps to understand your point of departure.

We face the same need when we begin to work with a new client. Having a profile of the current state of both the family and the business helps us do our work more efficiently and effectively. In Practical Tool #1, we provide an extract of three instruments we have designed and use at the beginning of each engagement:

- The Business Prosperity Profile
- The Six Transition Profile
- The Personal Well Being Profile

## Practical Tools 2 and 3
### *Conflict Resolution and Problem Solving Processes*

Conflict comes with the territory in family businesses and almost every day brings another problem to be solved. These two tools are intended to further your understanding of the differences between conflicts and problems, and how they occur. Beyond that, they provide step-by-step approaches for resolving conflicts and solving problems.

The best time to use these tools is the next time you are faced with conflict in the family or a tough problem in the business that you just can't seem to solve using the methods you currently have in place.

## Practical Tool 4
### *Family Charters*

Family Charters are documents that reflect the consensus reached by families about how they will manage specific elements of the relationship between the family and the business. Other terms that have been used for these documents include "Family Creed," "Family Business Policies," and "Family Business Constitution." Whatever you choose to call it, this morally binding document is an important guide to decision making in the future.

Your Family Charter should evolve over time as the result of thoughtful discussion and deliberation of selected topics. A portion of every family retreat should be devoted to developing and maintaining your Family Charter.

## Practical Tool 5
### *Family Councils*

The Family Council is the body that takes a leadership role in strategic development of the family/business relationship. Practical Tool 5 is a brief summary of the purpose, organization and operation of the Family Council. It is intended to give you enough information about whether this tool will work for your family business.

## Practical Tool 6
### *Family Meetings and Family Retreats*

Every family with children should be holding weekly family meetings. As the children reach adolescence and, later, as the family grows as the result of marriages, annual family retreats become important. This practical tool is designed to inform you about what you can do to make both family meetings and family retreats worthwhile uses of time.

## Practical Tool 7
### *Fundamentals of Family Business Compensation*

Compensation is an important subject in any business. In family businesses, the challenges of fairly and equitably compensating both family and non-family employees are particularly acute. This tool provides insight into the philosophy that provides the foundation for a sound compensation program, and suggestions for structuring a program in a family business.

## Practical Tool 8
### *Characteristics of Balance in Family Businesses*

Our experience has enabled us to isolate those 10 qualities that exist in successful family business systems and set them apart from the rest of the pack. Use this list as a guide to the goals and aspirations in your family business.

Assuming you have read parts 1 and 2 of *Hats Off to You — 2*, you know that we view family business succession as a lifelong journey. Common sense suggests that planning any journey is more productive if you first know your point of departure. We use three questionnaires with each of our clients to give everyone a quick read on how well prepared they are for the challenges they will be facing on their journey.

## Business Prosperity Profile

The first instrument is the Business Prosperity Profile. It is completed by all family members employed in the business, and by non-family employees in key management positions. It is comprised of 48 statements, six statements for each of the eight critical functions in which any successful business organization must excel.

Results of this Profile provide a snapshot of how effectively the business is currently performing relative to these functions. Examples of the statements contained in the Business Prosperity Profile include:

**Leadership:**
- We have clear, concise statements of vision and mission with which all members of management are intimately familiar.
- All family members in leadership positions have the knowledge, skills and abilities required for their roles.

**Management and Organization**
- Our wage, salary and incentive programs are equitable.
- Cross-department coordination works well, and we have an effective decision-making process.

**Finance**
- We have financial projections for revenue and profitability, and regularly review performance against those projections.
- The owners' desired return on investment (ROI) and/or return on equity (ROE) is defined. The business consistently meets or exceeds targets.

**Marketing and Sales**
- A marketing plan and budget are prepared annually and aligned with the strategic plan.

- We have an effective process for assessing our customers' needs and preferences, and responding to them.

**Operations**
- We are able to accurately determine costs and profits by product and/or service line. That system is driven by operations/production management.
- Standards for inventory levels and turns are thoughtfully established and regularly monitored.

**Innovation**
- We have an effective system for soliciting ideas, giving feedback, and recognizing and rewarding innovative recommendations.
- We have both budget and staffing for the development of new products and/or services.

**Quality**
- Our understanding of quality and service is based on knowledge of our customers' needs and expectations.
- Our quality program is documented and followed throughout the organization, and is not limited to operations/production.

**Communication**
- Our meetings are timely and effectively run (e.g., published agendas and minutes, facilitator/leader, follow-up process for action items, etc.)
- Reports generated by our management information system meet the needs of our individual managers regarding content, format, timeliness and accuracy.

**Each of the 48 statements can be responded to in one of 4 ways:**
- A. Our performance is fully acceptable. There is little or no need for attention/improvement.
- B. We are performing close to an acceptable level in this area, but there is recognizable room for improvement.
- C. Our performance in this area is well below an acceptable level—substantially less than our business requires.
- D. I do not know.

Each level of response is assigned a numerical value on a scale of 1 to 4 (A=4 to D=1). Results are provided in the form of a grade point average for each statement, each function and for the overall business.

## Six Transition Profile

The second of the three questionnaires is the Six Transition Profile. Each adult family member is asked to respond to 48 statements—eight statements about each of the six transitions in our family business succession planning model. These 48 statements reflect the most significant factors leading to successful succession planning. Examples of the statements contained in the Six Transition Profile include:

### Founder's (Current Leader's) Transition:

- The founder's (current leader's) continuing role in the business has been discussed with the next generation of management, and is well defined.
- The founder (current leader) and his/her spouse have diversified their asset base to the extent that their ownership in the business represents no more than 50% of their total assets.

### Family Transition:

- Our family has worked together to develop the individual and collective communication, problem solving and conflict resolution skills of all adult family members.
- We have considered, defined and documented the rights and responsibilities for each of the various business and family roles we play.

### Business Transition:

- We have an active, functioning Board of Directors or Advisory Board, with independent, non-family members.
- Rules for compensating family members employed in the business have been established and effectively balance business and family considerations.

### Management Transition:

- A timetable and deadline for selecting the successor(s) to the top management position(s) has been established and documented.
- We know where the authority rests for making management selection decisions.

### Ownership Transition:

- Every adult family member understands the rights, roles and responsibilities that apply to owners of our business.
- We have discussed and decided whether or not to offer ownership opportunities to non-family members.

**Estate Transition:**
- The estate plans of the founder (current leader) and all other family stakeholders are complete and are reviewed annually.
- Funding provisions exist for the payment of estate tax obligations.

**Each of the 48 statements can be responded to in one of 4 ways:**

1. Our current status is fully acceptable. There is little or no need for attention/improvement.
2. There is room for improvement. It is a high priority item. Our efforts should begin during the next 12 months.
3. There is room for improvement. However, in view of other priorities, improvement efforts should begin 13 or more months from now.
4. I do not have sufficient information/knowledge about this statement to express an opinion.

A compilation of the responses of all family members helps our clients and us get an initial understanding of:

- Priorities among the six transitions and 48 factors.
- Subjects on which the family generally agrees.
- Subjects on which the family has widely divergent viewpoints.

### Personal Well Being Profile

We designed this questionnaire to help individual family members discover the extent to which their needs are being met by the family business system. This is an exercise in self-discovery. As such, it is for the private use of each family member. Responses are neither returned nor scored. We do find, however, that when clients complete this instrument they gain a better sense of perspective about the need for balance between business prosperity, family harmony and personal well being. We often use this information when coaching individual family members.

The Personal Well Being Profile contains five elements.

1. Profession (purposeful activity within or outside the home)
2. Family
3. Self (self-awareness and self-satisfaction)
4. Social Responsibility
5. Financial Stability

Responses to each statement are on a five element scale and range from "Strongly agree" to "Strongly disagree," with an "Uncertain or Not applicable" option. Examples of the statements, which guide individual family members through this self-discovery process, are:

**Profession:**
- I have influence over decisions that affect me.
- I am on a path to achieving my work goals.

**Family:**
- I believe relations between family members are healthy and strong.
- Our family is clear about vision and values.

**Self Awareness and Self Satisfaction:**
- I am clear about my personal values and how I exhibit them in my day-to-day behaviors.
- I successfully deal with the conflicts I currently experience in my professional life.

**Social Responsibility:**
- I am comfortable with the causes my family supports.
- I am clear about my philanthropic goals.

**Financial Stability:**
- I understand my income and financial requirements.
- I am content with the level of financial returns from my ownership in the family business.

For information on how you can use the DHV Profiles in your family business or advisory practice, please contact the DoudHausner Vistar office either by phone to 818.539.2267, or by e-mail to admin@dhvadvisors.com.

## PRACTICAL TOOL #2
### Conflict-Resolution Process

### Background and Perspective

If for no other reason than the differences between business and family values (chapter 2), conflict is inevitable in a family business. We don't mean the potential for conflict. We mean that conflict is always around. It may be dormant or very low-key, but it is there. Want to see conflict? Here is a simple recipe for finding some conflict to observe:

- Put more than one person to work on any type of activity—business or pleasure.
- Require that they work together.
- Keep them working together long enough.
- Voila! Eventually you will observe conflict.

### Factors Influencing Conflict

How readily you recognize conflict, and how severe it might be, depends on a number of factors:

- Competence: Are all parties equally up to the task, or are some more competent than others? Sooner or later, the more competent may become frustrated by the less competent, and vice-versa.
- Difficulty: How complex is the task? Is this something that an individual of average intelligence could handle, or would it tax the abilities of a team of rocket scientists?
- Time pressure: How quickly must the task be done? Is the deadline consistent with the degree of difficulty? Getting something done in one month creates less time pressure than getting it done yesterday.
- Risk: What are the costs of error? If the stakes are high, there will be greater potential for conflict.
- Reward and recognition: How significant is the outcome? How much recognition is at stake? If the significance and recognition factors are low, then it should be relatively easy for the parties involved to worry less about power and more about purpose. If the future of the free world and the Nobel Peace Prize hang in the balance, watch out!
- Different interacting styles of the participants: Not everybody receives and processes information in the same manner. It is

important that differences in style are both understood and respected.

## Understanding Conflict

None of us can totally eliminate the sources of conflict, but we can learn to manage conflict when necessary. Realizing that most families dislike and avoid confrontation may help to keep the right perspective.

- Conflict is not always negative, particularly when those involved have developed skills to resolve their differences.
- Conflict can be an excellent reality check.
- Conflict becomes problematic only if it is left unresolved and grows in intensity.
- If your goal is successful conflict resolution, remember that if there is a "winner" and a "loser," you may have reached a solution but not lasting one. If it was a win/lose situation and you were the winner, watch out. The loser is waiting for the next opportunity for a "gotcha." Lasting resolution requires consensus. All parties must feel they are winners on some issues—hence the commonly used term "win/win negotiations." Our working definition of consensus is "a condition in which everyone's ox is gored, but the lance goes to the same depth in each ox."
- Each one of us has a unique personality—his or her own style and approach to getting things done; his or her own set of interests, sense of priority and emotional "hot buttons."
- Using that knowledge to help you appreciate and respond to the other person's point of view is productive. Using it for the fun of pushing "hot buttons" is disruptive. Don't!

## Steps for Successful Conflict Resolution
1. **Define the matter in conflict as specifically as possible.** We define "conflict" as the interpersonal and emotionally charged by-product of a "problem," which usually involves facts. If sales are falling, you have a problem. If you and your sales manager can't agree on what to do about it, the two of you are in conflict.
2. **Share individual perspective.** All parties to the conflict must have the opportunity to articulate their personal position and feeling. They should then be able to share what they believe to be the other position and feelings of the other involved.

This is an important step. The conflict may be based on nothing more than incorrect assumptions about another's position. If that's all there is to it, resolution shouldn't be far away.

3. **Acknowledge differing points of view.** The intensity of conflict often can be reduced simply by one person having his or her position and feelings acknowledged and validated. You don't have to agree with them, but you have no basis for denying their right to their opinions or disregarding feelings. *("That's a stupid way to feel." "You can't think that way.")* No matter how dysfunctional it may seem to you, it is the other person's reality. Acknowledge it!

4. **Identify possible areas of agreement.** It is a safe bet that you aren't 180 degrees apart on 100% of the matter in conflict. Certainly there must be some common goals, shared perceptions, mutual interests. Find them! Things will go better once you do.

5. **Define the desired outcome.** What does success look like? If you can't describe it, you'll have a hard time finding it.

6. **Focus on observable behavior.** What specific behaviors would the other party need to display in order to aid in the solution of the present conflict—and avoid fixture conflict over the same issue? These behaviors must be described in operational terms. Saying "treat me with more respect" is not a clear request for a change in behavior. Ten people would have 10 different examples of respectful behavior as they interpret it. What does "respectful" behavior look like to you? If you can't describe it, how can another person know what he or she is committing to do?

7. **Avoid finger pointing.** You're in conflict. You both already know each of you thinks it is the other person's fault. There is no point in beating a dead horse. *"It's your fault." "No it isn't, it's your fault. " "No it isn't, it's your fault. "* This is a nonproductive conversation that is bound to lead nowhere.

8. **Share responsibility for change.** If all parties to the conflict really want to end the conflict, then all should be willing to contribute to resolution. What one change in behavior are you each willing to make to help reduce the conflict? Once these changes are articulated, both parties can begin changing. When the conflict has gone down a notch you can get together again to see about the next notch.

9. **Evaluate progress.** Set aside time at regular intervals to review

progress. Recognize successes and be realistic about shortfalls. Be supportive of each other. Change is often difficult. What can you do to help your colleague over the rough spots?

10. **Be realistic.** Success requires unanimous commitment from all parties. Without that, lasting resolution is a dream, not a reality. If resolution is not possible, your are responsible to yourself. Determine what you must do to change your attitudes and responses in order to live with the situation.

### Regarding Implementation

We know many families that have become so good at this process that they no longer need outside assistance. Few started that way. If you are new at this, don't try it on your own. We have heard more than one story of a self-facilitated meeting that was intended to resolve conflict. Instead, the meeting got nasty, tempers flared and the conflict got worse. Find and use a skilled outside facilitator. The mere presence of a neutral third party helps keep negative outbursts under control. Make sure that the person you select:

- Understands both the family and business implications of your conflict;
- Is someone with whom everyone has good personal chemistry;
- Is someone you trust!

## Problem Solving Process

On page 153 we provided a working definition of the difference between a problem and conflict. We have observed that the term "problem" is used when facing an objective issue. The term "conflict" is usually reserved for interpersonal issues. This process is designed for problems. Try it on for size in your next management meeting. You will find that it works!

1.  Define all aspects of the problem by getting everyone's answers to the question: *"What do we have?"* List the answers on a flip chart and hang them on the wall.

2.  Define what the desired condition looks like by soliciting answers to the question *"What do we want?"* Again, record the answers.

3.  The next question is "What could we do?" Brainstorm. Think freely about any and every possible way to get from what you have to what you want. Remember, in brainstorming there are no "wrong" ideas. Get everything out. Don't discourage creative thinking by being judgmental. You can sort it all out later.

4.  Question number four is *"What will we do?"* Go back to the brainstorming results. Discuss options and select those that have the support of the group.

5.  Once you have determined what you will do, fix responsibility for implementation. The operative question to be answered here is "Who will do it?"

6.  A. If the responsible person has all the authority he or she needs to tackle the problem, then let them get on with it. Skip Step 6 and move to Step 7.

    B. If he or she needs approvals along the way, then they will need to prepare an action plan and budget for review and approval.

7.  Set a follow-up date for feedback and evaluation of progress.

8.  Evaluate progress on the date you established in Step 7. If the problem has been solved, celebrate. If issues remain, review the action plan. *"What needs to be done differently?" "What can you do to help achieve a more effective result?"*

Experience has shown over and over that a systematic, structured approach to problem solving is the best way to accomplish the desired results.

# PRACTICAL TOOL #4
## Family Charters

In chapter 2, "The Family Transition," we discussed the importance of reaching consensus on the process for managing the family's relationship to the business. This is a major part of your quest for balance between business prosperity, family harmony and personal well being.

It is hard work. Deciding on equitable "rules of conduct" isn't easy, particularly when the discussions must focus on such issues as how family members will be treated with respect to:

- Employment in the family business
- Compensation
- Performance management
- Ownership

That is just a partial list of obvious issues that exist in every family business. The list for your family may be longer.

Solutions that meet a wide variety of needs must be thoughtfully developed. It's a healthy process but can go on for a long time. That is why we recommend documenting the family's decisions as they are developed. The advantages are twofold:

1.  You don't have to trust that everyone will remember each decision the same way months and years after it was made. (They won't!)

2.  The document makes it easy to explain the rules to someone who wants and needs to know. A good example is the family member who was in her early teens when the decisions were made, is now graduating from college and is wondering what she can expect from the family business.

This document has been given many names. We prefer "family charter" because it is a statement of the shared principles governing the family's relationship to the business. We encourage each of our clients to write a family charter as they move along on their succession journey in search of balance.

It is an evolutionary document. In the typical setting, at least one element of what will eventually become the family charter is on the agenda at every family retreat. (See Practical Tool #6 for a discussion of family meetings and family retreats.)

On the following pages we have provided a couple of samples for you to study. They are actual family charters developed by two of our clients. We thank them for their permission to reprint them here. (In respect of their rights of confidentiality, we have changed the names and eliminated any reference to the names of their businesses.)

They are effective family charters; not because they adhere to any empirical standard, but because they meet the needs of the families that developed them. We are not suggesting you copy them. They may not be "right" for your family and your business. And, as useful as these samples may be, the process of developing the family charter is as important as the resulting document.

## STATEMENT OF PRINCIPLES
## A GIFT FROM THE SECOND GENERATION
## TO THE THIRD GENERATION
## JANUARY, 199X

To our children and their spouses:

We are proud of our accomplishments. Over the past 25 years, we have nurtured and grown the business started by your grandfather. We have known bad times and good. We have known happiness and heartbreak. We have worked our way through our share of disagreements about the business, maybe more than our share.

As we move closer to placing responsibility for and ownership of this business into your hands, we want to share with you those principles that have served us well over the years. They worked for us. Living by these principles kept our family and its business healthy, brought some of you into the business and kept others out.

We cannot be sure what principles you will decide to apply. We do know that we committed these to writing late in our careers, and wish we had done it much sooner. The process of codifying the principles and values by which we lived brought us closer together. We hope that you will see fit to start earlier than we did to determine the principles that will work for you. Make the commitment, take the time. No matter how much you may struggle, it will be worth it. Good luck and God speed.

— Signed by the members of the second generation

### OWNERSHIP

1.  Family members should be free to be owners, or to sell all or part

of their investment in the company. We support the definition of a variety of possible levels of involvement of family members as owners, and support freedom of choice among these possibilities. We believe that individual commitment should derive from choice.

2.  Every effort will be made to develop assured cash flow to all investors in return for having put their capital at risk in the family business. However, the reasonable financial needs of the company must first be met. Those needs will be determined by management and the board of directors.

3.  We will strive to eliminate family pressures from ownership decisions of family members.

4.  Too sudden a withdrawal of capital could be damaging to the company. Therefore, we have created mechanisms that will allow individual investors maximum flexibility in the withdrawal of funds without placing an unreasonable burden on the company.

5.  We recognize that the family will have an impact on the values that drive our business. We encourage continued, thoughtful family participation in this endeavor.

6.  We pledge to maintain a strong, positive family influence on the business.

7.  We encourage the equity participation of those family members who choose to remain as owners.

## GOVERNANCE

1.  The second generation has created a board of directors of the company to represent the interests of ownership. All owners have the right to vote on board representation proportional to their share of total ownership. They also have the obligation to act responsibly in exercising that right.

2.  The bylaws provide for appropriate ownership participation in deciding significant policy issues (e.g., mergers, sale of all or part of the company, significant changes in capital structure). Owners have an obligation to the business and to each other to be responsible and knowledgeable participants in those decisions.

3. The company's board of directors consists of a mix of individuals who can provide appropriate perspective on governance of the company. At all times, the board should include:
   a. Individuals who occupy key managerial positions
   b. Individuals who represent significant ownership interests in the company and who are sufficiendy dedicated, interested and able to do the homework necessary to provide meaningful input
   c. Individuals from the outside business and professional world who will bring valuable experience and fresh perspective to the company

4. The governing board will not be involved in day-to-day management issues.

5. Board members who do not work for the company will be fairly and equitably paid for their services.

## EMPLOYMENT OF FAMILY MEMBERS

1. Family members have the freedom to follow their own career paths. There is no compulsion to join the company and, when making a choice of employment, individual family members should consider the best utilization of their interests and talents.

2. Extra effort will be made to give family members who wish to join the company the support necessary for them to meet normal employment standards and be accepted by the company.

3. Sound employment procedures will not be compromised in employing a family member. Hiring and promotion decisions will be made on the basis of an assessment of the relative qualifications of all candidates to contribute to the success of the business.

4. Family members who work for the company must recognize the pressures inherent in the situation, which make it critical for them to maintain satisfactory performance.

## FAMILY ORGANIZATION

1. We encourage the continuance of family meetings to support effective governance and the work of the family in the preservation and development of corporate principles.

2.  Each individual family unit is of primary importance. We will not compromise the family for the business, nor the business for the family. We recognize that this is easier said than done.

### GENERAL PRINCIPLES

1.  Family members are encouraged to continue to give back to the community their time, talent and money.

2.  We support this Statement of Principles and continued effort by the Third Generation to improve it.

## THE JONES, SMITH AND TUCKER FAMILIES
## OUR RESPONSIBILITY TO OUR BUSINESS
## AND TO EACH OTHER
## AUGUST, 199X

### GENERAL PRINCIPLES

We believe that family ownership, governance and management of our business have been the key to our success and profitability. This has enabled us to maintain the reputation for quality, service, and fairness that we enjoy among our customers, employees and suppliers. Therefore, we are unanimously committed to maintaining ownership, governance and top executive management of our business in our family for the foreseeable future.

We recognize that our various roles (family member, owner, manager) each make different demands of us. We firmly resolve to keep these differences in mind and approach every problem or issue on the basis of the kind of issue it is—a family issue, an ownership issue or a management issue. We are committed to making businesslike decisions on any matter that involves or impacts our business in any way.

### OWNERSHIP

- Ownership of our business will be restricted to bloodline descendants and legally adopted children.
- Any family member may own stock in the company. Voting stock may be held only by those family members who are actively involved as members of management.
- Family members who leave the management group will be required to convert any shares they own to nonvoting stock.

The procedures are documented in our shareholders agreement.

- Family members may sell their stock back to the company at any time in accordance with the price and terms specified in our shareholders agreement.
- A word about pricing philosophy: We want to make sales of stock possible in case of need, but do not wish to encourage the practice. A valuation of the business will be made every other year by a qualified independent valuation firm, and will include applicable discounts for lack of control and lack of marketability. We have agreed that the sale price will be 50% of the price determined by the valuation firm.
- A word about the philosophy behind terms of sale: We agree that terms must be fair to the seller but must not place undue financial pressure on the company. Terms may change from time to time as conditions warrant, and will be defined by a majority vote of our independent directors.
- It is our intent to pay dividends of an equal per-share amount to holders of both voting and nonvoting stock whenever warranted by the profitability and reinvestment needs of the business. Dividends will be declared by the board of directors. No family member will consider dividends to be a guaranteed source of income. The financial well being of our business comes first.

## EMPLOYMENT

- We encourage active participation by family members in the management of the company. However, employment in the company is not a birthright; rather, it is a privilege to be earned based on the qualifications of the individual and the needs of the company.
- A college degree is required of any candidate for consideration for any supervisory or management position. There will be no exceptions. We pledge to provide each family member the financial support to complete an undergraduate degree program (and graduate degree program if desired) at the college or university of his or her choice.
- Family members may be considered for employment in non-supervisory and nonmanagement positions at any time, and are encouraged to take advantage of this opportunity to gain exposure to the company during their high school and college years.

- In addition to a college education, we require at least two years' work experience (including supervisory experience) outside the family's business before any family member applies for employment at a supervisory or management level.
- Family members employed by the company will be compensated fairly. Salary and bonus opportunities will be consistent with the competitive marketplace and internal relationships to other positions. Actual individual salaries and bonuses paid within the range of opportunity established for each job will be as merited by individual performance.
- The performance of all family members employed in the company will be regularly evaluated in the same manner as for all nonfamily-member employees. In the event of substandard performance, family members will be subject to the same disciplinary standards that apply to all employees—up to and including dismissal.

## GOVERNANCE

- The strategic and policy direction of the company will be the responsibility of the Board of Directors. The family and management will be represented on the Board, which will also include at least two independent directors. Qualifications for family members and outside directors are as follows:
  — Owners who are not active in the business but who have the interest and ability to understand business information and make sound business decisions;
  — Selected outsiders who possess knowledge and expertise that will add dimension to the board's decision-making capability.
- Board members who are not employed by the company in another capacity will be compensated for their service at both Board and committee levels.

## MANAGEMENT

- Our company's success is directly dependent on the core values that drive it. The overall guiding principle under which we work is to treat all people with whom we come in contact (customers, employees, suppliers, members of the community in which we live and work) with dignity and respect.
- Everyone (family and nonfamily) involved in any way in

ownership, governance and/or management roles is expected to maintain the core values and guiding principles of this company at all times. Family members in active management roles bear a special responsibility for this.

- We will consistently adhere to sound management principles in all decisions made and actions taken on behalf of the company.

## GENERAL

- As owners of our company, we will do our best to conduct ourselves in our personal lives in ways that bring credit to our family and our company.
- We recognize that we will face differences of opinion from time to time. We pledge to respect the feelings and opinions of each family member (whether or not we agree with them), to communicate openly and honestly with one another and to work toward achieving consensus in the decision-making process.
- It is the family's responsibility to meet annually to review this statement and to make whatever changes are required to improve it and/or make it more responsive to the needs of the family and the business at any given time. Annual family retreats will include time for working on the business; time for education to make us better; more responsible owners; and time to play together and enjoy the fellowship of our family.
- It is the family's responsibility to take the time to stay informed about the business.
- It is management's responsibility to make sure that family members have the information they need to meet their responsibilities to our business.

★ ★ ★ ★ ★

This document is the result of three years of effort. It reflects the commitment that every member of this family has to both the family and our business. More importantly, it reflects the love we have always felt for each other, and the trust in each other that we had to build to make this a reality. We promise to make this a living document by revisiting it every year. Any part of it can change if there is consensus for that change. In the meantime, these are the rules by which we will conduct our family/ business affairs.

— Signed by each adult family member

We have repeatedly mentioned the importance of communication, problem solving and conflict resolution in a balanced succession process. Business prosperity, family harmony and personal well being don't just happen. They are the results of hard work and dedication over time. Family councils are an important part of achieving and maintaining balance in family businesses.

**Question:** *"When is a gathering of family members not a social event?"*
**Answer:** *"When it is a family council meeting."*

The term "family council" has become very popular in the past few years. It has received so much press that we often receive calls from family businesses looking specifically for help in setting up their own family council. They have heard that it is something important to family businesses, and they want one. The next words out of the caller's mouth are usually, "By the way, just what is a family council?"

The family council is a group of adults representing the family and meeting regularly to work on two fronts:

1. Achieving and maintaining balance between business prosperity, family harmony and personal well being.

2. Finding the "success" in family business succession.

The family council is, in effect, a wholly owned subsidiary of the family. It is the organization in which adult family members come together to work on strategic planning for the family. Members of a family council are part of the same group that gets together from time to time to celebrate birthdays, anniversaries and holidays. But they are brought together as members of the family council for a different purpose.

Effective businesses conduct regular management meetings to review and evaluate operating results. They are the nerve center for the "business of the business." The family council accepts a similar role in dealing with the "business of the family." Their goal is to achieve the family/business balance to which this book is dedicated.

Establishing a family council is an exercise in organizational development. As such, the most important matters that require attention are:

• Charter
• Membership

• Authority

Your family will need clarity about each of these subjects. Beginning on the next pages are ideas to guide you in developing a family council in your family business.

Charter—Defining the purposes of the family council
- To bring adult family members into shared responsibility for creating balance in the family/business relationship
- To provide a forum for free and open discussion of the family's responsibility in support of business prosperity, family harmony and personal well being
- To help ensure that business ownership is a unifying force in the family rather than a divisive one
- To ensure that the family is well informed in family business matters, and competent to use and interpret the information they receive
- To provide a forum for voicing questions and concerns
- To provide a venue for dealing with conflict resolution

Membership—Defining the right to participate
- Who should serve? Family councils are typically representative of the entire family population (age groups and branches). Consider rotating terms for younger adults and permanent terms for elder statespersons.
- Will your family council include in-laws? We believe it should. They, too, have a direct stake in the council's work.
- Will you limit family council membership to those who are active in the business? We would not advise it. They already have management meetings. This is about the family's relationship with and responsibility to the business.
- 

Authority—Setting boundaries for the family council
The family council should be:
— A forum for expressing ideas, building understanding and developing competence.
— A vehicle for establishing a consensus on the rules that will govern the family's conduct in its relationship with the business and to each other.

- The family council should not have any decision authority on matters within the purview of ownership, executive management or the board of directors. (However, in some families the council has the right to express opinions on strategic business matters before the board.)

## PRACTICAL TOOL #6
### Family Meetings and Family Retreats

## Terminology

This Practical Tool covers both family meeting and family retreats. They are different activities. We define the difference as follows:

- Family Meetings: These are most appropriate for individual family units. They take place on a regular schedule, require only an hour or two and are held at home.

- Family Retreats: Retreats are better suited to families with two or more branches and/or two or more generations of adults. They are 1½ to 3-day events held off-site in a retreat/conference setting. They have broader agendas, include family members of all ages, and combine a variety of business and family topics and activities.

## Family Meetings

When children are young, we encourage using weekly family meetings to develop healthy communication patterns. The guidelines for these weekly meetings are:

1. Establish and maintain a regular schedule.
2. Set a specific time limit for meetings and stick to it.
3. Prepare an agenda. Agenda items should provide both for airing concerns and acknowledging positive achievements.
4. Encourage all family members, regardless of age, to suggest topics to be discussed during the meeting.
5. Rotate the responsibility for chairing meetings among all family members.
6. Establish rules of conduct and communication.
7. Make it the responsibility of the chair to enforce the rules.
8. Give every family member a voice in deciding what the rules should be. Write these rules on a chart that is displayed at every meeting. Examples of conduct and communication rules include:
   - Family members will be treated with the same courtesy and consideration we give to our closest friends and our most important customers/clients.
   - No yelling, name-calling or making insulting remarks.
   - The speaker will not be interrupted.
   - Every family member will be given a fair share of time to talk.

9.  As the children grow, their schedules will become more complicated. There may come a time while children are still living at home to change from weekly to monthly—or quarterly—meetings.

10. Also as the children grow, the agenda of the family meetings may evolve to include a greater focus on the family's business.

## Family Retreats

Managing the family/business relationship is a never-ending responsibility. When regular family meetings are no longer feasible, the annual family retreat becomes the venue for maintaining focus on that relationship. It is an opportunity for the entire extended family to spend a few days together in a casual, relaxed atmosphere. It is a time for learning together, talking together and playing together. Family retreats play an important part in keeping both the family bonds and the family/business relationship strong and healthy.

## Seven Possible Purposes

As indicated above, family retreats can serve many purposes in the family business system. While not every retreat needs to serve them all, over time your family can use them to your advantage in the following seven ways:

1.  Heighten the family's awareness of the family business: In a typical family business system, each family member can be identified as belonging in one of four categories:

- Active; Informed
- Inactive; Informed
- Active; Under-informed
- Inactive; Under-informed

One important purpose of family retreats is to eliminate underinformed family members. Families with members who can identify with—and feel personally connected to—the business find it easier to maintain continuity through generations than families in which this quality is absent.

2.  Keep the family connected to each other: Families grow. Children marry and start their own families. Some may move away. Some enter the family business while others do not. Despite these changes, the vital link between the family and the family's business goes on.

Family retreats are particularly effective in helping bridge the gaps created by change. Many of our clients have fond memories of growing up together, but are scattered throughout the country They use family retreats to keep those memories alive, and to allow cousins to come together and create tomorrow's fond memories of their extended family. A feeling of emotional connection can pay dividends in later years.

3. Nurture a climate that supports effective communication: Use family retreats to build and practice communication, problem solving and conflict resolution skills. Open, honest communication is an important key to effective successions and continuity.

4. Establish and maintain clarity of vision and unity of purpose: Every family should recognize the importance of a clearly articulated statement of the family's vision for the future and of its relationship to its business. That vision statement can make unity of purpose a living reality. And unity of purpose can unleash the very positive power of the family business. A family retreat is a perfect setting to establish a statement of vision that can then be reinforced at all future family business activities.

5. Education and skill building for family members: Retreats should be viewed as opportunities to build knowledge and competence needed for effective family/business relationships. Determine what knowledge and skills family members need to be responsible owners of the family's business and stewards of its legacy. Use family meetings and retreats to transfer the knowledge and build the skills.

6. Establish the "rules" governing the family's relationship to the business and to each other: The concept of a "Family Charter" was presented and discussed as Practical Tool #4. Charters are typically created over a number of family retreats. Use part of one retreat to establish the content outline for your Family Charter. Use part of each subsequent retreat to deliberate about, decide on, and/or review at least one item in your Charter.

7. Celebrate your family and your family business: Every family re-

treat should contain some activities that celebrate the joyful side of owning and operating a family business. The list of possibilities is limited only by your imagination.

## Retreat Agenda

Each family retreat should provide opportunities for planning, problem solving and education. Suggested agenda items include:

- Workshops to develop such personal and group skills as communication, problem solving, conflict resolution and public speaking.
- Learning the history of the family business.
- Creating a family vision statement and mission statement.
- Developing the Family Charter by reaching consensus on the rules that will be used to guide the family's relationship to its business, e.g., rules for:
  - Employment of family members
  - Compensating family members employed in the business
  - Performance management for family member employees
  - Requirements of responsible business ownership
  - The role of in-laws in the family business
- Family governance.
- Reading and interpreting financial statements.
- Understanding the key operational and financial aspects of the family business.
- The family's responsibility to the community(ies) in which it does business.
- Philanthropy.
- Estate planning techniques.
- Responsible financial stewardship/investment management.
- Career options both within and outside the family business.

## Recreation/ Celebration

No matter what else is on the agenda, each family retreat should include time for recreation and celebration. Some families have held golf, tennis, volleyball and horseshoe tournaments. Others have organized horseback rides or hay rides and held chili cook-offs. Some have staged a "Family Olympics" with games in which all generations can participate— and followed that with an awards banquet. Organize a family talent show. Spend an evening sharing the family's history. Show a video of last year's retreat. Watch a video history of the family business. The recreation and celebration opportunities are limited only by your imagination.

## Retreat Mechanics

Here are some guidelines that will help you plan your family retreats.

1. Location: Get away from routine surroundings. Retreat may be held at such varied locations as resorts, a beach house or mountain cabin, or a cruise ship. "Away" can be 10 miles from home or 1,000. The "right" location is anyplace that the family agrees is fun, comfortable and affordable. One family with business locations in 6 different states rotated their retreats and used resorts close to a different one of their business locations each year. Part of the retreat agenda included a tour of the facility.

2. Scheduling: The larger the family, the greater the scheduling challenge. Scheduling the same weekend each year gives family members time to clear their calendars. One of our clients holds their family retreat on the weekend closest to the founder's birthday. Another uses the weekend nearest the anniversary of the business.

3. Planning: It is a good idea to assign responsibility for planning the retreat to family members not active in the business. If your family has a Family Council, that is a logical place for responsibility to rest. If you have a Family Office, the staff can arrange for accommodations, meals, meeting rooms, audio/visual support, travel, contract ing with outside resources, etc. However, the responsibility for agenda planning and development should stay with the family.

4. Chairing the Retreat: This responsibility can be rotated among family members. It is another good opportunity to involve family members not active in the business. Additionally, the use of a professional facilitator can greatly enhance the effectiveness of the entire activity.

# PRACTICAL TOOL #7
## Fundamentals of Compensation for Family Business

Compensation is, at best, a difficult and highly emotional subject. Like it or not, one of the most prevalent measures of success used in our society is how much money one makes. In that atmosphere, even the most sound, well thought through compensation decisions made—and actions taken—by competent, responsible leaders and managers will not please everyone all the time. Moreover, this year's decisions and actions will be all but forgotten next year.

That challenge, however, is not an excuse for leaders and managers to throw up their hands and abrogate their responsibility for making sound compensation decisions. In the face of the complications mentioned above, a fair and equitable reward system designed around sound compensation philosophy can be a powerful motivational and retention tool. Conversely, a system built on top of a faulty philosophical base can be demotivating to employees and disruptive to the business.

In family businesses the compensation design and management challenge is particularly acute when the family-based value of "equality" and presumptions about entitlement lock horns with the business-based values of *"fairness," "equitability,"* and *"differentiation."*
The principles provided in this Practical Tool reflect sound compensation philosophy. They have been tested over many years in thousands of businesses—and have withstood many challenges. We encourage you to study them carefully. They may challenge some approaches to compensating family members that have existed in your family business for many years. If they do, then adopting new principles and practices will take courage. However, we believe that if they are adopted and supported they will make an important contribution to business prosperity, family harmony and personal well being. Accordingly, they are worthy of your wholehearted and unanimous support.

## How Compensation is Earned

There is an important distinction between how compensation is delivered to managers, and how it is delivered to owners. Managers and other employees are rewarded by compensation in various forms, and by benefits and perquisites. These rewards become operating expenses of the business.

Owners are rewarded by "dividends." That word is in quotes because we know that for tax purposes family businesses often work hard to avoid dividends in the formal sense. Nonetheless, it is important to keep in mind that whatever the means of delivery, everything an owner receives when wearing his/her owner's hat is a "dividend." Dividends are the "leftovers." They are available for distribution after operating expenses are paid and necessary reinvestment capital is provided to the business.

Whereas employee compensation depends on job value and personal performance, ownership rewards depend on business results and percentage of ownership.

## The Compensation Pyramid

Effective compensation programs are built from the bottom, up. The construction sequence is illustrated in the diagram on this page. The pyramid shape is significant in that in most family businesses, going from the bottom up, each succeeding element represents a smaller percentage of total compensation. Sound design philosophy considerations for each element of the program are discussed below.

Pyramid levels from top to bottom: S.E.B / Long Term Incentives / Perquisites / Annual Cash Incentives / Benefits / Base Compensation

### Base Compensation
### General Comments

Sound design principles begin with base compensation. It forms the base of the pyramid for a number of reasons:

1. It is the single most significant source of cash income for most (if not all) employees.
2. Participation in many benefit programs, and in incentive plans, is typically expressed as a percentage of base salary. Therefore, if base salaries are not "right," an organization's compensation program can be built on an unsound foundation and will lose much of its reward, motivational and retention value.

## Setting Base Compensation Opportunities

There are two considerations to be balanced when establishing a range of base salary opportunities for each position in the organization:

1. External Competitiveness: Each position has a value range relative to other similar positions in the appropriate employment area, e.g. national, regional, local. The range for any job in any organization must be set to allow you to compete effectively for qualified candidates for that job. Set it too low and you will get what you pay for. Set it too high, and you will overspend on compensation— thereby denying the organization needed working capital and/or downgrading the owners' return on their investment.
2. Internal Comparability: Each position contributes in different measure and in different ways to the business. Some supervise more people than others (line responsibility). Some have greater policy setting authority than others (functional responsibility). Some have greater decision authority than others and—as a result—impact business performance more direcdy. Some require more experience and/or more "technical" knowledge than others. Understanding the relative "worth" of positions with the organization is essential to establishing the range of salary opportunity for each position.

Taking both external competitiveness and internal comparability into account enables management to fairly distinguish between salary opportunities provided to jobs of varying "worth." Failure to make these distinctions will cause employees whose salary is set too low to become disaffected. Employees whose salary is set too high will become defensive. The typical net result is a dysfunctional, under-performing business.

### Setting Individual Compensation

Salary opportunities are best expressed in ranges with a minimum and a maximum, and further divided into quartiles between those two extremes, as illustrated here.

The positioning of an individual's base pay in the salary range when the person is hired depends upon his/her qualifications. How the employee progresses through the range depends upon his/her performance. General points of design philosophy which guide the effective use of salary ranges are as follows:

**Minimum:** That level below which you will probably not attract qualified employees to your business.

| MAXIMUM |
|---|
| 4th Quartile |
| 3rd Quartile |
| —MIDPOINT— |
| 2nd Quartile |
| 1st Quartile<br>MINIMUM |

**1st Quartile:** The hiring range. That range of compensation at which the business can effectively attract employees possessing minimum qualifications for a particular job.

**2nd Quartile:** Advanced hiring and growth opportunity range. Businesses use this quartile to hire employees with greater than minimum qualifications. Good compensation policies require approval from one level above the hiring manager to offer a new employee starting compensation in the 2nd quartile. This quartile also provides opportunity for salary growth for employees in the 1st quartile. A good employee who is hired with minimum qualifications typically improves at a high rate. Accordingly, merit increases tend to move good employees through the first quartile and into the second quartile rather rapidly.

**Midpoint:** This is the "control point."
- No employee should be hired above the midpoint without approval from two levels above the hiring manager.
- In the theoretical ideal, an employee who consistently meets all the performance requirements of his/her position should be compensated at the midpoint.
- In the aggregate, good compensation management strives to create a situation in which the base compensation of all employees in the same salary range averages out at the midpoint.

**3rd Quartile:** This quartile is used to recognize consistent performance at levels above expectation. Movement through the 3rd quartile will be slower than movement through the 1st and 2nd because the rate of improvement will slow down as an employee learns more. (It is very much like learning a sport. A novice will become an average player much more quickly than an average player will become a "pro. ")

*NOTE:* In a well-managed salary structure, most of the employees in a given range will be paid in the 2nd and 3rd quartiles.

**4th Quartile:** This is a "safety valve." In most middle market organizations the practical limits of job advancement may create a difficult situation. A very good employee has no opportunity for promotion, but his/her employer wants to retain that employee. This is the best use of the 4th quartile. Sound compensation policies consider compensation in this quartile to be an exception that requires two levels of approval.

**Maximum:** If you are paying above the maximum, you are wasting money! That said, exceptions can always be made, but they should be thoughtfully made against defined guidelines.

## Merit Increases and Cost of Living Adjustments

The primary way an employee moves up within the salary range for his/her job is through merit increases. Although rarely mentioned, there are really two considerations when deciding on whether to grant a merit increase. The first is improvement in performance since the last compensation review. The second is demonstrated sustained performance over time. They go hand-in-hand. However, the longer an employee stays in a particular job, the more weight sustained performance carries. This is true because, as mentioned above, the rate of improvement will decrease over time.

## Equality and Equitability; Employees and Owners

Many family businesses try to maintain compensation equality among family members. When businesses are first formed the management/ownership team is usually very small. That small group of pioneers shares multiple responsibilities in a scary, exciting, informal, "whatever it takes" environment. In the early years of a business, there is often little thought given to the distinction between how owners are rewarded for the work they do and how they are rewarded for taking ownership risk.

As these businesses grow, the size of the management team typically increases. The organization becomes more complex. Individual responsibilities become more specialized. Differentiation develops between levels of job responsibility and impact on the business. Also, as the business continues into succeeding generations, the number of owners typically increases and not all of the new owners are necessarily active in the business.

This increased complexity calls out for more formality in the organization and in all the management systems of the business—including compensation. In larger organizations, similar positions may be grouped in the same salary grade and share a salary range. In smaller organizations, each position may have its own range. No matter, in well-managed businesses there will be differentiation between salary opportunities available for different jobs. It also calls for the owners to make explicit distinctions between compensation and "dividends."

## Benefits

If for no other reason than the high cost of individual access to various types of insurance coverage (medical, disability, life) the availability of lower-cost group benefits makes this element of compensation extremely important. In addition to insurance-based benefits, retirement-oriented benefits (retirement savings plans, pension plans, etc.) are typically an important element of a total benefits plan.

Therefore, base compensation alone is not sufficient to make your business a competitive employer that is able to attract and retain high caliber employees. The benefits package must also stand up to those offered by other employers.

For the purposes of this discussion, we are talking about qualified benefits, i.e., benefits plans which meet federal standards to be includable as a business expense. Because of the relationship between compensation levels and benefits levels inherent in many of these regulations, it is essential to have a sound, equitable base compensation foundation upon which to add this second building block in the compensation pyramid.

## Annual Cash Incentives
### *Why Provide Annual Cash Incentives?*

The terms "base compensation" and "fixed compensation" can be used interchangeably. Base compensation is usually fixed for a year at a time. It is paid for past performance in anticipation of equal or better future performance. Employees receive base compensation in return for delivering expected performance, i.e., for delivering performance that provides owners with a reasonable return for having put their capital at risk by investing in the business.

Annual cash incentives are based on the philosophy that owners are willing to share that portion of their returns that exceed their expectations with the employees who helped create better than expected returns.

### *Why Not Use Discretionary Bonuses?*

Many family businesses like to use discretionary bonuses. Under such a system, each year the owner decides what cash bonus "feels" right. It is highly subjective. If there is more than one owner, then two or more people have to negotiate their individual subjective judgments and try to reach consensus. Negotiating on feelings rather than facts is cumbersome, time consuming, and often approached with some fear and trepidation by all parties.

Under this system employees get some money each year. They usually don't know why they get it or how the amount was determined, but they come to expect it. In that regard, a discretionary bonus is very much like the monetary equivalent of the "Christmas turkey." In this paternalistic approach to compensation, the owner(s) may feel good about being generous. But there is substantial downside risk. How does one explain why this year's bonus is less or more than last year's? How does one explain why one employee got more and the next employee less? ("Hey, I worked harder than she worked.") How does one explain that there is no bonus this year?

## Why Use Performance-Based Incentives?

There are substantial advantages to a performance-based incentive plan:

1. Guesswork is eliminated: Owners and participants know up-front both what levels of performance will generate incentive rewards and what rewards will result at various performance levels. That, alone, generates an incentive value that is absent in discretionary bonus plans.

2. Objectivity replaces subjectivity: The terms of the plan are definable and defensible. This facilitates decision making.

3. It is risk free to owners: Expected levels of ownership return are locked in before incentive rewards are made. They are paid as a portion of better-than-expected returns.

## Basic Design Concepts

1. Reward Company-wide and Individual Achievements: Business success requires that every manager pulls his/her own oar, and that they all pull together. Using an incentive plan that rewards both company-wide (team) and individual accomplishments sends the right message.

2. Define Two Measures of Company-wide Performance: Two measures work better than one because they can provide balance. As an example, measuring sales growth but not profitability may send the message of "sales growth at any cost in profit." Doing the opposite could send a message of "profit at any cost in sales." Neither is a good message. Measuring both sends a message that profitable growth is the goal. Both the measures and the performance targets are subject to annual change—and one or both may well change as business conditions evolve.

3. Set Targets for Company-wide Performance Measures: The target levels for the measures of company-wide performance are those which provide for 100% funding of the incentive pool. If you believe that full funding of incentive awards should be provided for exceeding expectations, then the target levels should be higher than

the budgeted levels of expected performance. Should you elect to provide full funding for meeting expectations, then target levels should be the same as the levels specified in the operating budget. We generally recommend the first approach.

4. <u>Establish a Performance Threshold</u>: It is highly unlikely that actual year-end performance will be precisely as planned. It may be better than expected, or it may not meet expectations. Well-designed plans allow for reasonable deviation from the target by funding the incentive pool at levels greater or less than 100% of target. However, responsible leaders and managers set a minimum threshold below which no incentive awards are made. It is all about protecting owners' returns.

5. <u>Define Measures of Individual Performance</u>: The top executive has company-wide responsibility for performance. Everyone else contributes to overall company performance through his or her work in one or more functional areas. So everyone but the top executive should have 2 or 3 annual performance measures and targets. Both measures and targets should be reestablished annually, and may well change. Today s most important areas for individual achievement may be replaced by others as conditions change.

6. <u>Specify the Incentive Opportunities</u>: Each person should have a target incentive expressed as a percentage of base compensation. Targets typically vary by organization level. Typically, individual incentive targets are set within the following ranges:
   - Top executive target 50 - 75% of base salary
   - 2nd tier executives   30 - 50% of base salary
   - 3rd tier executives   10 - 25% of base salary

If company-wide performance funds more than 100% of target, a participant could earn a reward greater than the target. If company-wide performance funds less than 100% of target, a participants opportunity could be less than the target.

This is illustrated in the matrix example on page 170.

7. <u>Distinguish Between Awards</u>: Some portion of the target should be rewarded directly based on company-wide (team) performance. The rest should be based on performance against individual performance targets. The top executive's reward is based totally on company-wide performance. Successively "lower" management tiers have relatively less impact on the overall performance. Thus,

individual performance makes up a larger share of their total incentive award. For example:

| Management Level | Pct. For Company-wide Performance | Pct. For Individual Performance |
|---|---|---|
| Top Executive | 100% | -0 |
| 2nd Tier Manager | 60% | 40% |
| 3rd Tier Manager | 40% | 60% |

8. Communicate the Award Structure: Let all participants know what is possible. This is most readily done through a matrix. A purely hypothetical example is provided below. In this example 100% of the sales target is $37MM, and 100% of the profit target is 14%.

| $ Sales / Profit Pct. → | 12 | 12.5 | 13 | 13.5 | 14 | 14.5 | 15 | 15.5 | 16 |
|---|---|---|---|---|---|---|---|---|---|
| $48 - 50MM | 0 | 120 | 130 | 140 | 150 | 160 | 170 | 180 | 190 |
| $46 - 48MM | 0 | 110 | 120 | 130 | 140 | 150 | 160 | 170 | 180 |
| $42 - 44MM | 0 | 100 | 110 | 120 | 130 | 140 | 150 | 160 | 170 |
| $40 - 42MM | 0 | 80 | 100 | 110 | 120 | 130 | 140 | 150 | 160 |
| $38 - 40MM | 0 | 60 | 80 | 100 | 110 | 120 | 130 | 140 | 150 |
| $36 - 38MM | 0 | 40 | 60 | 80 | 100 | 110 | 120 | 130 | 140 |
| $34 - 36MM | 0 | 0 | 40 | 60 | 80 | 100 | 110 | 120 | 130 |
| $32 - 34MM | 0 | 0 | 0 | 40 | 60 | 80 | 100 | 110 | 120 |
| $30 - 32MM | 0 | 0 | 0 | 0 | 40 | 60 | 80 | 100 | 110 |
| Less Than $30MM | 0 | 0 | 0 | 0 | 0 | 0 | 0 | 0 | 0 |

Percent of Pool Funded

**Examples of Incentive Payment Calculations**

The following examples illustrate how the incentive payment for a hypothetical executive would be calculated under three different combinations of company and individual performance. For purposes of these examples, the executive has:

- A base salary of $80,000
- A target incentive of 40 percent of base
- An incentive that is based 60 percent on company performance and forty percent on individual performance.

## Example 1 — Company Performance on Target: 100% Pool

1. Percent of pool funded     100%
2. Base Salary     $80,000
3. Target award (as % of salary)     40%
4. Available award (1x3) x 2     $32,000
5. Percent of award from company performance     60%
6. Percent of award from individual performance     40%
7. Performance as percent of individual targets     80%

Company performance award 5x4     $19,200
Individual performance award (6x7) x 4     $10,240
Total Incentive Award     $29,440

## Example 2 — Company Performance Below Target: 80% Pool

1. Percent of pool funded     80%
2. Base Salary     $80,000
3. Target award (as % of salary)     40%
4. Available award (1x3) x 2     $25,600
    (32% of salary)
5. Percent of award from company performance     60%
6. Percent of award from individual performance     40%
7. Performance as percent of individual targets     90%
Company performance award 5x4     $15,360
Individual performance award (6x7) x 4     $9,216
Total Incentive Award     $24, 516

## Example 3 — Company Performance Above Target: 120% pool

1. Percent of pool funded     120%
2. Base Salary     $80,000
3. Target award (as % of salary)     40%
4. Available award (1x3) x 2     $80,000
    (48% of salary)
5. Percent of award from company performance     60%
6. Percent of award from individual performance     40%
7. Performance as percent of individual targets     100%
Company performance award 5x4     $23,040
Individual performance award (6x7) x 4     $15,360
Total Incentive Award     $38,400

## Perquisites

Perquisites (or "perks") provide ways to deliver non-cash compensation at higher levels of management. However, under today s tax codes, perks do not generally allow recipients to avoid paying taxes on the value of perks received. Indeed, some perks (such as club dues) are not deductible by the employer as a business expense.

We are not qualified to provide tax counsel relative to the use of perks. The most commonly used perquisites include:

- Automobile or auto allowance
- Auto maintenance
- Club memberships
- Payment of spouse travel to business events
- Company-paid income tax preparation
- Company-paid financial/investment advisory services

## Long Term Incentives

One of the shortcomings of performance-based annual cash incentives is that they focus attention on short-term results. A fully matured total compensation plan will provide long term incentives to encourage key executives to make decisions with a mind to the balance between the short- and long-term consequences of those decisions.

Public companies typically use stock options. Family businesses rarely do. Other avenues for providing long-term incentives can include phantom stock, and deferred compensation. Insurance-based programs can be used to fund deferred compensation.

Of course, long-term incentives can't be implemented unless longterm goals are in place. Thus, the presence of a good strategic business plan is a prerequisite to designing and utilizing long-term incentives as part of a total management compensation program.

## Supplemental Executive Benefits

Some companies find that the limitations on qualified plans do not allow them to provide key executives with the level of benefits they would like. When that is the case, supplemental executive benefits can be employed. Some simple examples include:

- Payment of health insurance deductibles
- Insurance coverages such as vision care and dental care that may not be offered under qualified plans
- Additional pension benefits.

Although to our experience these are not widely used in family businesses, those owners and/or executives responsible for developing the total compensation program should be aware of their availability.

## Retirement Compensation For the Senior Generation

One of the most troublesome compensation challenges facing family businesses is meeting the income needs of the generation that is phasing out of 100% participation in management. Most retiring owners want to maintain the lifestyle to which they are accustomed, and they have gone through life assuming that the business will continue to pay them full salary—even though they are working less (or not at all). Ideally, the retiring owner(s) would have done some retirement planning and developed independent sources of retirement income. But the reality is usually far from the ideal. The senior generation frequently faces the future with little more than a dependence on continuing payments from the business to sustain them.

From the point of view of the successor generation, this unfunded obligation can be a real burden. In many family businesses, the number of families depending on the business for a livelihood grows in each generation, and the business needs to reinvest in itself to remain vital. Funding retirements out of operating income can be close to unaffordable.

On the other hand, the founder's (or current leader's) rationale is simple. It often takes the following form:

- *"I founded (or built) this business."*
- *"I was considerate and generous when I provided employment opportunities to my sons, daughters, nieces and nephews."*
- *"I could have sold the business and lived handsomely off the proceeds, but I chose not to because I wanted them to have opportunities."*
- *"Surely I deserve some reward for all this?"*
- *"Oh, by the way, whatever we do, I want to be able to live comfortably and minimize my income risk."*

Like it or not, that is a pretty good rationale. The members of the senior generation do, indeed, deserve to be rewarded for their years of hard work and, often, sacrifice, building business value. If that reward is not going to come from an amply funded retirement plan, what are the options? One possibility would be for the seniors to accept drastically reduced income levels. Having said that, we've yet to meet anyone who is anxious to do that. That leaves two possibilities: Sell stock to successors or adjust the rationale for compensating the out-going generation.

## Sell Stock to Successors

One possibility is to sell stock to members of the successor generation and reinvest the proceeds. That may need to be part of the answer, but it has some drawbacks and limitations:

- For a number of reasons the senior generation may feel uncomfortable without voting control. That places a practical limit on the amount they are willing to transfer.
- The successor generation may not be able to afford to buy the stock. Most often the successors are younger men and women, often with young families and little discretionary income.
- It isn't very tax efficient. Buyers pay tax on the funds used for the purchase, and sellers pay tax on the gains realized by the sale. If tax efficiency is a consideration, gifting stock over time is a better approach. However, it doesn't put any money in the pockets of the people making the gifts.

## Adjust the Compensation Approach

The best hope for family businesses caught with unfunded retirement obligations is to develop a new rationale for and approach to compensating the senior generation as they play less and less of a role in the business. Without regard to dollar amounts, here is an approach that has been successful in many family businesses. It won't absolve the senior generation of all risk, but it can keep the risk they must take within acceptable limits.

**First, establish a total compensation target for the senior generation:** Senior generation members should expect that their total compensation will drop somewhat as their level of involvement subsides. The goal is to find a target that respects the needs of the business as well as the needs and desires of the senior generation. It might be wise to use the services of a competent financial planner to help assess target income levels.

**Second, reduce the level of fixed compensation:** Continue to pay salaries or consulting fees, but at a lower level than the senior generation members were receiving when working full time.

**Third, provide a share of profits on a preferred basis:** Allocate a portion of the profits of the business to augment the senior generation's fixed compensation. Guarantee them a preferred position that is calculated after incentives are paid to non-family employees, but before payment of incentives to the successor generation. If the business is a subchapter S corporation, the amount of this portion of compensation will depend upon expected pass-through reportable income based on ownership percentages. In general, the higher the ownership percentage, the lower will be this third component of the unfunded retirement compensation program.

This is not a perfect solution. It doesn't totally absolve the senior generation of business risk, and it doesn't avoid the need to allocate annual operating revenues to an unfunded retirement income program. However, in the absence of a funded retirement program it is far better than merely picking a fixed number out of thin air and sticking to it regardless of how the business performs.

## Characteristics of Balanced Family Business

The reason for setting goals is to define success. Over the years we have observed that family businesses in balance demonstrate certain qualities. We hope that in them you will find the goals to which you and your family aspire.

### 1. Flexibility

Although families love the status quo, they are not static entities. Children become adults, parents age, and the family grows as in-laws arrive and grandchildren are born. Individuals make diverse lifestyle choices. Family traditions evolve—sometimes gradually, and sometimes not so gradually.

In balanced family businesses, family members have learned to remain flexible. They adapt to today's realities. They cherish yesterday's memories but are not mired down in them.

### 2. Shared Values

It can be challenging to define values, but family businesses in balance know the values that drive their business and their family. Moreover, they share that value system. It is very important to talk about values. Such conversations help family members learn what others care about. You will find that there are typically more similarities than differences, even with the proverbial "black sheep" in the family.

Try this simple exercise at your next family retreat:

- Ask each person to list the three aspects of family life that he or she values the most.
- Permit each person to share his or her selections and discuss why they are his or her favorites.
- When the sharing is done, compare everyone's top three picks. Find and discuss the similarities and the differences.

This exercise will open up important sharing that can enhance your understanding of one another concerning values.

### 3. Effective Communication Skills

Balanced families have overcome their predisposition to avoid confrontation, no matter the personal price they pay. They have learned, practiced and mastered the techniques of effective communication, problem solving and conflict resolution. They bring issues to the table as they occur, and deal with them together until a mutually satisfactory resolution is in hand. They hold regular, facilitated family retreats and use outside resources to help hone their communication skills.

## 4. Respect for Personal and Professional Boundaries

In balanced family businesses:

- Every family member knows which hats he or she owns and does not own.
- The roles and responsibilities that come with each hat have been discussed and are known to everyone.
- Family members do a very good (not perfect, but very good) job of wearing the right hat at the right time—and not trying to wear hats they don't own.
- Business disagreements are left in the office; family disagreements are left at home.
- Time is consciously set aside to allow some family time without interference from the business, some business time without family interference, and some personal time without interference from either business or family.

## 5. Loyalty and Sense of Belonging

Balanced families stay close by choice, not by demand. This is possible when:

- Family members know how to support each other.
- They want to support each other.
- Family traditions exist that work for everyone.
- Family members learn to build on their similarities and value their individuality.

## 6. Empowerment

Families empower individual family members when they encourage and support each other's dreams and aspirations. It takes knowledge to be supportive. Do not assume that you really know someone just because the two of you are members of the same family. How well do you know the hopes, fears and dreams of the other members of your family?

## 7. Quality Time

Balanced families are those whose members find more positives than negatives about each other. That enables them to enjoy the times they are together, in both the business and family settings.

In the business, each person carries his or her own weight in whatever roles he or she plays. In the family, it is a joy to be together rather than a chore or obligation.

## 8. Spiritual Wellness

"Spiritual" does not refer to any specific organized religion. We simply find that families who share a belief in a higher power have an advantage. They are more likely to have shared values. A family with a healthy spiritual life will find it easier to get into balance—and to stay in balance.

## 9. Ability to Apologize, Forgive and Forget

The family business was being sold because two brothers could simply not find a way to coexist, even after two years of good-faith effort. On the day of decision, one brother said, *"When I was ten and he was eight, he lied to Dad and I got into trouble. He never apologized. Even though he has not done that again, I have never been able to trust him in business."*

There are three important lessons to be learned from this true story.

1. Eric Segal wrote *"Love means never having to say you are sorry."* Don't believe him! Love means learning to say *"I'm sorry,"* and meaning it.

2. People will do things that are hurtful and inconsiderate. That is human nature. Instead of dwelling on it, figure out what lessons you have learned and move forward. A sincere apology will make that somewhat easier.

3. Be willing to make fresh starts. What happened in the past cannot be undone. We can, however, have something to say about the present and the future.

## 10. Strategic Family and Business Planning

Family businesses in balance take their strategic future seriously. They know and share the vision and mission for the family and the business. They use that shared knowledge to strengthen their family/business relationship. Goals and action plans are in place in both the family and the business. Implementation is a reality, and progress toward goals is measured.

## *Acknowledgments / 1st Edition*

We did not create this book in a vacuum.

The first group of people we want to thank and honor are our professional colleagues and friends who put a bit of themselves into *Hats Off to You* by their encouragement, ideas and constructive feedback.They are, in alphabetical order: Alan Boal of Able Navigator International; Patrick L. Burns and Edwin S. Cox, Ph.D., two of our colleagues at DoudHausnerVistar and Associates; Douglas K. Freeman, Esq. of Freeman, Freeman and Smiley; David L. Goldstein of Pacific Life; Richard L. Pumilia, Esq. of Pumilia, Adamec & Stevens; and Julie Shifman, Esq.

Our special thanks to the many family businesses we have had the privilege of serving during our careers. These have been wonderful associations. On the one hand, we have worked hard to help our clients achieve the balance they need to find the success in family business succession. On the other hand, they have provided us the experiences that have shaped our perspective on family business and enabled us to be responsible students of our profession.

Finally, we acknowledge the professional advisors in so many disciplines who have worked with us on behalf of the clients we mutually serve. Responsible consulting to family business clients is a multidisciplinary effort. We have benefited from working on many teams with some highly skilled professionals.


HATS OFF TO EACH AND ALL OF YOU!

## *Acknowledgments / 2nd Edition*

We remain deeply indebted to all those who helped us create the 1st edition of Hats Off to You. The acknowledgement text from that edition is as current today as it was then, and is reprinted in its entirety below.

In addition, we thank our partner Rachel Mickelson and two more of our professional friends. Michael Roney of Roney Financial - First Financial Resources in Pasadena, CA. and Bill Weintraub, a tax and estate planning attorney in the Century City office of Jeffer, Mangels, Butler and Marmaro. Rachel contributed her perspective on strategic business planning. Mike and Bill shared their time and expertise with us in reviewing what we have written about the Ownership and Estate Transitions. We are grateful for their contributions.